JOHN LENNON

A PHOTOGRAPHIC HISTORY

JOHN LENNON

A PHOTOGRAPHIC HISTORY

SARAH RICKAYZEN   MARIE CLAYTON   GARETH THOMAS

ATLANTIC PUBLISHING

Atlantic Publishing
38 Copthorne Road
Croxley Green
Hertfordshire
WD3 4AQ

© Atlantic Publishing
Concept and Creative direction Atlantic Publishing

First published by Atlantic Publishing in 2011
This updated edition published 2020
Photographs © Associated Newspapers Archive complemented with photographs from Getty Images.
See page 224 for details.
Front Cover © Robert Whitaker

Paperback: 978 1 909242 88 3

Hardback: 978 1 909242 81 4

Printed and bound in China

Contents

Introduction

John Lennon was the man who brought us The Beatles, and whose energy and commitment to becoming "bigger than Elvis" was greatly influential in taking them to the heights. He was a man of many contradictions – a superstar who came to hate fame; a singer who didn't like the sound of his own voice; a devoted husband who was often unfaithful. His song writing partnership with Paul McCartney changed the parameters of popular music, and his early prose writing added to the richness and diversity of the English language.

When The Beatles were at the height of their fame, John was known as the thoughtful, intelligent one; celebrated for his sharp wit and swift put-downs. After they broke up, he moved away from commercial music and went on to create a new and exciting career in his own individual way. His relationship with Yoko Ono became one of the great love stories of our times, and with her he developed into both an interesting conceptual artist and an influential campaigner for Peace. After an intense period of experimentation, his music also developed and matured, with his songs reflecting both his philosophy of life and his sharp observation. Despite his talent and commitment to the world of the arts, when his son Sean was born he took five years out of the public eye, dedicating himself to raising his child.

John Lennon: A Photographic History charts the fascinating life of this complex and charismatic man, right from his Liverpool beginnings to his tragic death in New York. The exciting collection of photographs not only show him performing, but also include candid shots documenting his private life. The photographs are accompanied by detailed captions which give a rounded portrait of the world's first superstar peace campaigner. John Lennon was a phenomenon and his legacy continues to fascinate people even today. He was always a larger-than-life figure, but he has become a true cultural hero of our times.

CHAPTER ONE

THE EARLY YEARS

With love from me to you

John Winston Lennon was a man full of contradictions: often aggressive, with a caustic wit and cutting tongue; against authority and determined to go his own way despite all opposition; but also surprisingly gentle, generous and sometimes deeply sentimental. Much of his complex nature was formed by his troubled and insecure early years – as was revealed in many of his later songs. His mother, Julia, was a cinema usherette when she met and married Alfred Lennon, known as Fred, a ship's steward. Within months of their wedding, Fred was back at sea and although at first he wrote fairly regularly and sent money back, his continual absences severely strained their marriage. Predictably, Fred was at sea when John was born on 9 October 1940 and later his home leave became increasingly erratic and his letters less frequent. Julia was young and attractive, and she was not prepared to sit at home and wait for a missing husband. A brief affair led to the birth of a daughter, who was quickly adopted, but soon afterwards she met and fell in love with John "Bobby" Dykins, a hotel waiter, and she and the young John moved into his small flat.

Since Julia was still married, the family were horrified and her eldest sister, Mimi, who was married but childless, came to take John away. At first Julia refused to let him go, but when the social services department became involved she gave way and John was whisked off to Mendips, the comfortable home of Mimi and her husband George, in Menlove Avenue, Woolton.

For a while John's life settled down. Although she was a strict disciplinarian, his aunt had adored him since he was born, and his uncle enjoyed having a surrogate son. John could always rely on Uncle George to play with him, provide encouragement or to bail him out of trouble. He did not lose touch with his mother, as she came to visit him every day. However, in July 1946 Fred Lennon appeared on the scene again, and persuaded Mimi to allow him to take John to Blackpool for the day. Fred Lennon reportedly planned to vanish with his son to New Zealand and start a new life, but Julia came rushing after them. The five-year-old John witnessed his parents arguing over who was to have him, and then Fred asked him to choose who he wanted to live with. It was an impossible situation – he loved his mother, but longed to have his father around. At first John chose Fred, but when Julia left he went running after her in tears. Julia carried him back to the safety of Mimi's house and it was to be many years before John saw his father again.

Julia settled with Bobby Dykins and they had two daughters, Julia and Jacqui. They lived quite near Mimi's house, and John got on well with his two half-sisters and accepted Bobby, so he visited regularly but continued living with Mimi. When he started school he did well and, although he was obviously an individual, he stayed out of trouble at first. It was soon after he started at Quarry Bank School, aged eleven, that the problems began. Quarry Bank was a

Opposite: The Beatles return from Sweden in 1963.

more authoritarian environment, but John quickly decided he did not respect the teachers. It also became apparent that he was very short-sighted, but he hated wearing his glasses so he usually couldn't see the blackboard. On top of all this, in 1955 his beloved Uncle George died suddenly of a haemorrhage. Although John was obviously bright, he lost interest in lessons, began skipping school, swearing and smoking, his grades dropped and he soon had a reputation as a troublemaker. Mimi was worried and upset but could do nothing to change his attitude.

Meanwhile, John had begun to see more of his mother. Julia was very different from her serious sister – she was headstrong, always smiling, looked down on authority and loved practical jokes. She could play the banjo a little and she taught John a few chords. He soon became seriously interested in music, encouraged by Julia but to the despair of Mimi, who could see no future in it. John and Julia both admired Elvis Presley, and John adopted the "teddy boy" look. He also started his own skiffle group, first called The Blackjacks but soon renamed The Quarry Men. It was when The Quarry Men were playing at a church fête in July 1957

that John met Paul McCartney for the first time. Paul came from a musical family and could already play the guitar well, so he was soon invited to join the group.

After leaving Quarry Bank School John started at Liverpool College of Art in September 1957. Despite his interest and ability in art he did little better there than he had previously, because now he was determined to let nothing get in the way of his interest in rock 'n' roll. At college John became very friendly with Stuart Sutcliffe, a talented artist, and persuaded him to join The Quarry Men, while Paul introduced George Harrison to the group. It seemed that John had finally found a direction, but he was soon to be struck by another blow. In July 1958, on her way home from Mimi's house, Julia was struck by a car as she crossed the road and killed instantly. The death of his mother, whom he had come to regard very much as a kindred spirit, devastated John so badly that he was unable to talk about the loss for many years.

Many students at the college remember John's striking individuality, and girls usually found him very attractive. He had several girlfriends, but soon became seriously involved with Cynthia Powell. Their relationship seemed unlikely, as Cynthia was from the upmarket side of the Mersey, had been strictly brought up and was quiet – almost the total opposite of John – but the attraction was instant and mutual. They soon had a profound influence on each other; John gave up the "teddy boy" look and adopted a more conventional appearance, while Cynthia took note of his obsession with Brigitte Bardot, and proceeded to dye her hair blonde and dress more provocatively.

By 1960 The Quarry Men had changed their name to The Beatles and were developing musically and even earning some money, but the turning point came in August that year when they were offered an engagement in Hamburg. After quickly enrolling Pete Best as drummer, the five of them left for Germany. In Hamburg they met Astrid Kirchherr, who cut their hair into the famous "moptop" style, and in the course of several visits over the next two years the distinctive Beatles sound was developed and honed. Stuart soon left the group, to stay in Hamburg with Astrid and concentrate on his art, but he and John remained close; so John was devastated when Stuart died suddenly of a brain haemorrhage. He had lost yet another important person in his life.

Left: George, John and Paul, the three permanent members of The Quarry Men, outside Paul's house in early 1960. That same year, John had recruited Stuart Sutcliffe to play bass and a few months later, Pete Best became the band's drummer. The five of them set off for a 15-week stint in the night clubs of Hamburg under their new name (via The Silver Beetles) of The Beatles. It was to be another two years before Ringo Starr joined and the line-up was finalized.

By the end of 1961 The Beatles were beginning to make an impact around Liverpool. Local record-store owner and businessman Brian Epstein offered to manage them and John accepted on their behalf. In mid-1962, after a great deal of hard work, Epstein achieved a recording contract for the fledgling group with EMI, but EMI's George Martin expressed concerns about Pete Best's drumming. John did not hesitate – telling Epstein that it was up to him to fire Pete; he himself went off to invite Ringo Starr, whom they had met in Hamburg, to join them as drummer instead. The Beatles' line-up was complete. There was also a big change in John's personal life at this time – Cynthia was pregnant and on 23 August they were married at Mount Pleasant Register Office in Liverpool. Aunt Mimi refused to attend the wedding but Brian acted as best man and both Paul and George were among the guests.

In October 1962 The Beatles had one record out and were due to appear on their first London TV programme, but they were still almost completely unknown outside Merseyside. Throughout 1963 they worked a punishing

Above: A leather-clad Lennon performing in the Cavern Club in December 1961. The band had returned from Hamburg late in 1960 and played at local venues around Liverpool, making their debut as The Beatles at the Cavern in February 1961. It became a regular and frequent venue for them, where they made over 290 appearances. It was here that record-store manager and would-be impresario Brian Epstein first saw them perform in late 1961; two months later he took over management of the band.

Above: The house where John Lennon was raised by his indomitable Aunt Mimi, 251 Menlove Avenue, Woolton, known as Mendips. This semi-detached 1930s house is opposite a golf course and around the corner from Strawberry Fields. John was the only Beatle to grow up in a middle-class suburb. It was decided that his devoted, but Bohemian, mother couldn't take the responsibility for raising her son and John went to live wth Mimi, her sister, but Julia often came here. Tragically, after one of her visits in 1958, she was killed by a car while hurrying across Menlove Avenue, a tree-lined dual carriageway, to catch a bus, John was just 17. When The Beatles made it big Mimi used to show fans around the house, inviting them in for tea and sandwiches.

schedule, which included four national British concert tours, two Scottish tours, one short Swedish tour and numerous one-night engagements. They also attended numerous photographic sessions, press interviews and radio and TV recordings. They began the year supporting Helen Shapiro, but gradually they became the major attraction.

The Beatles were busy in the recording studio too. Their second single, "Please, Please Me" was released in January, and the album of the same name followed two months later. Three further singles, "From Me To You", "She Loves You" and "I Want to Hold Your Hand", all reached the No.1 spot in the UK charts and the year ended with the release of a second album, *With the Beatles*, which remained in the top spot for 21 weeks, displacing *Please, Please Me*, which had occupied the position since May. There was more joy for John in 1963 when Cynthia gave birth to their son, John Charles Julian, in Sefton Hospital on 8 April. However, since John was away on tour at the time, it was several days before he managed to return to Liverpool to see his son.

In October 1963 a live appearance by The Beatles on the network TV show, *Val Parnell's Sunday Night at the London Palladium,* led to crowds of hysterical fans gathering outside the normally staid theatre in London. This caught the attention of the national newspapers, and from then on Beatlemania gripped the nation. When John, Paul, George and Ringo arrived back at London Airport from a short tour of Sweden a couple of weeks later, they were stunned by the thousands of fans who had gathered in the rain to welcome them back.

Towards the end of 1963, The Beatles were invited to appear at The Royal Variety Performance. John was determined to have a dig at royalty at the event, and made his famous and irreverent remark, "Would the people in the cheaper seats clap your hands, and the rest of you, if you'll just rattle your jewellery." The year closed with John and Paul being described as "the outstanding English composers of 1963" in *The Times*. Right from the start they had agreed between themselves that whoever wrote the songs, everything would carry the names Lennon-McCartney as composers. Neither of them realized just how significant this was to become.

Below: The Beatles, now with Ringo Starr on drums and their permanent line-up complete, posing with their instruments in a small backyard in London in 1963. The previous year, at the behest of George Martin, EMI's record producer, Pete Best had been fired. John had asked Ringo, whom they had met in Hamburg where he was performing with Rory Storm and The Hurricanes, to take over on drums.

Above: John displays the mop-top haircut and smart suit that were to become a trademark for The Beatles. Their gruelling schedule of working the northern theatres and ballrooms, as well as residencies at the Cavern Club in Liverpool and the Star Club in Hamburg, was giving the band the exposure they wanted. 1962 was a turbulent year for John – Brian Epstein had secured The Beatles a recording contract with Parlophone, a subsidiary of EMI, and their first single had been released; John had secretly married his long-term girlfriend Cynthia Powell and was looking forward to fatherhood. But the highs were marred by the death of John's close friend, and erstwhile band member, Stuart Sutcliffe of a brain haemorrhage in Hamburg in April.

JOHN LENNON TIMELINE: 1940 – 1962

1940

Oct 9 John Winston Lennon is born to Julia and Alfred Lennon at the Oxford Street Maternity Hospital, Liverpool. Alfred is absent.

1941

John is primarily cared for by his aunt and uncle, Mary (Aunt Mimi) and George, at 251 Menlove Avenue, Woolton.

1942

Apr John's father leaves home, having been away at sea for much of the time since his son's birth. Julia moves in with a new boyfriend, John "Bobby" Dykins.

1945

Sept John attends school at Dovedale Primary, Liverpool.

1946

Jul John is taken to Blackpool by his returning father, who intends to keep his son in his custody. Julia eventually locates the pair, and John decides to return to his Aunt Mimi's in Liverpool.

1952

Jul John leaves primary school.

Sept After passing the eleven plus exam, John starts Quarry Bank High School.

1955

5 Jun John's Uncle George dies.

1956

Skiffle music is popularized by Lonnie Donegan, and John's interest leads to the acquisition of his first guitar.

1957

Mar John forms The Blackjacks skiffle group, soon to be renamed The Quarry Men.

24 May The Quarry Men make their debut public performance at a street carnival, Roseberry Street, Liverpool.

9 Jun The Quarry Men fail to qualify for Carroll Levis' *TV Star Search*, held at the Empire Theatre, Liverpool.

Jul John leaves Quarry Bank High School.

6 Jul John meets Paul McCartney for the first time, when The Quarry Men play at St Peter's church summer fête.

20 Jul Paul joins The Quarry Men.

7 Aug The Quarry Men make their debut at Liverpool's Cavern Club.

Sept John enrols at Liverpool College of Art, where he is to meet his future wife, Cynthia Powell, and future Beatle, Stuart Sutcliffe.

1958

6 Feb George Harrison joins The Quarry Men, having watched them perform at Wilson Hall, Liverpool.

15 Jul John's mother Julia is killed by a car while crossing the road outside Aunt Mimi's house.

1959

29 Aug The Quarry Men perform at the opening of the Casbah coffee club, run by the mother of The Beatles future drummer, Pete Best.

15 Nov The Quarry Men briefly change their name to Johnny and the Moondogs and make the final audition for *TV Star Search*.

1960

10 May The Quarry Men become The Beatals.

20-28 May The group tour Scotland in a support slot as The Silver Beetles.

2 Jun They perform at Neston Institute as The Beatles.

Jul John leaves art college.

Aug The Beatles secure a stint in Hamburg, Germany, playing gruelling sets at the Indra and the Kaiserkeller, where they meet Ringo Starr.

5 Dec John returns to Liverpool after four months in Hamburg. George had been deported shortly before, for being under-age, and Paul and Pete Best were asked to leave having been accused of starting a fire.

1961

9 Feb The group play their first Cavern Club gig as The Beatles, performing in a lunchtime slot.

21 Mar The Beatles' first evening performance at the Cavern Club.

Apr The Beatles return to Hamburg. Stuart Sutcliffe leaves the group to focus on his art studies.

Jun "My Bonnie", a single by Tony Sheridan, is released in Germany, featuring backing by The Beatles.

6 Jul John contributes an article, "Being a Short Diversion on the Dubious Origins of Beatles", to the first edition of Liverpool music paper *Mersey Beat*.

1 Oct John and Paul holiday in Paris for two weeks.

28 Oct Local record-shop owner, Brian Epstein, learns of The Beatles' existence from fans enquiring about "My Bonnie".

9 Nov Brian Epstein attends a Beatles' performance at the Cavern Club.

Dec Brian Epstein offers to manage The Beatles; John accepts on their behalf.

1962

1 Jan The Beatles audition for Decca in London, recording fifteen tracks. Although the audition is to prove unsuccessful, Brian Epstein is later to use the recordings to cut a demo for EMI.

24 Jan The Beatles sign a management contract with Brian Epstein, although at this stage Epstein does not sign himself.

8 Mar The Beatles make their radio debut, recording at the Playhouse Theatre, Manchester, for BBC radio's *Teenager's Turn (Here We Go)*.

10 Apr Former Beatles' bassist, John's close friend Stuart Sutcliffe, dies of a brain haemorrhage in Hamburg, at the age of twenty-one.

13 Apr The Beatles make their third trip to Hamburg, securing a residency at the new Star-Club until the end of May.

9 May Brian Epstein secures a contract for The Beatles with Parlophone, a subsidiary of EMI. He notifies the group, who are in Hamburg, with a congratulatory telegram.

4 Jun Brian and The Beatles are signed to EMI, recording their first session at Abbey Road studios two days later.

15 Aug Ringo Starr, drummer with Rory Storm and the Hurricanes (who had also built something of a reputation through playing in Hamburg), is invited to join The Beatles as it is suggested that Pete Best lacks sufficient skill for recording work. Best is fired the following day.

18 Aug Ringo joins The Beatles, making his debut at Hulme Hall, Port Sunlight.

23 Aug John marries Cynthia Powell at Mount Pleasant Register Office, Liverpool. Cynthia is pregnant.

4 Sept The Beatles return to Abbey Road for their first formal recording session. Ringo is present, but due to an oversight, producer George Martin had invited session drummer Andy White, and subsequently it was White who was to drum on the first single, "Love Me Do".

1 Oct Brian Epstein signs a five-year management contract with The Beatles.

5 Oct "Love Me Do", backed with "P.S. I Love You" is released as The Beatles' first single.

17 Oct The Beatles make their television debut, performing live on the regional Granada programme *People and Places*.

26 Nov The Beatles record their second single, "Please Please Me".

> "I was sitting at home one day just thinking about what a good name the Crickets would be for an English group. The idea of beetles came into my head. I decided to spell it BEATles to make it look like beat music, just as a joke." — **John**

Do you want to know a secret?

Opposite: John backstage in 1963. Despite his apparent confidence, made more evident by his outspokenness and willingness to engage, he had nagging self-doubts, particularly about his singing voice, which he disliked. He was always asking George Martin, The Beatles' producer, to "do something with it" – to make it sound like something other than his own natural voice.

Top left: Mainstream success arrived in 1963, with the four attracting attention wherever they went; but not all the publicity was positive – John made headlines in the *Daily Mirror* after beating up Bob Wooler at Paul McCartney's 21st birthday party, when the Cavern Club DJ insinuated that the relationship between John and Brian Epstein was more than a professional one.

Middle left: The Beatles return from a short tour of Sweden in late 1963 to be met by thousands of screaming fans and the press at London Airport. Waiting for a flight to the US is Ed Sullivan, the American TV host, who witnesses Beatlemania for himself. Having found out more about the group, he soon contacts Brian Epstein to book the band for his CBS show the following year.

Left: The Beatles gained massive exposure from their TV debut on *Thank Your Lucky Stars* in January 1963. Backstage, John sips tea and relaxes with the rest of the group. Later in the year he makes his solo TV debut on *Juke Box Jury*.

Below: Already beginning to feel the strain of a busy schedule – with six tours, a host of one-night shows, numerous photo-shoots and press interviews as well as recording commitments under their belts – the boys find time to relax with a new racing-track range from Scalextric.

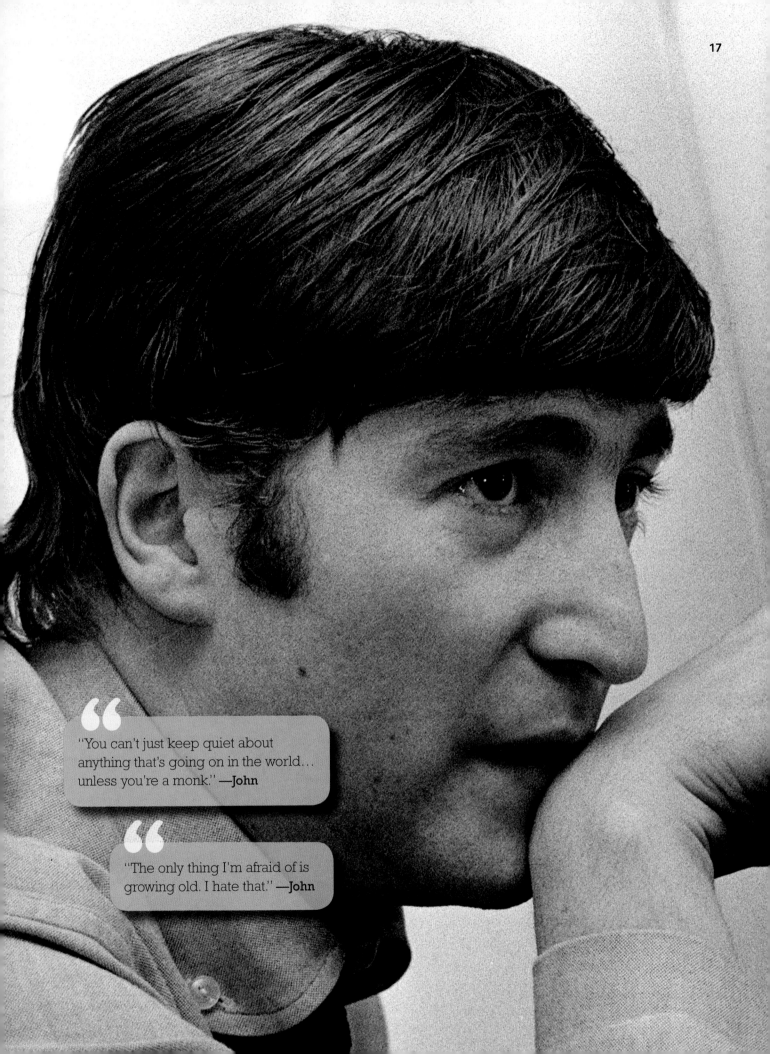

"You can't just keep quiet about anything that's going on in the world... unless you're a monk." —**John**

"The only thing I'm afraid of is growing old. I hate that." —**John**

Celebrated wit

Left: Beatlemania hit the Royal Variety Performance in 1963, where the band were caught on camera "jumping for joy" during rehearsals. John's title of "the most outspoken Beatle" became apparent once more when, on stage during their set, he uttered his celebrated witticism: "...would the people in the cheaper seats clap your hands, and the rest of you, if you'll just rattle your jewellery." Brian Epstein was reportedly pleased when the audience's response was applause and laughter; he had pleaded with John to say something less offensive than he had originally intended.

Left inset: During an early performance by the Beatles, John and Paul share a microphone as they harmonize in what became their trademark performance style. As friends and song-writing partners, they were a fine example of opposites attracting one another. John's troubled childhood and stormy teenage years contrasted strongly with Paul's "ordinary" upbringing. Despite, or perhaps because of, their differences they had a unique ability to write songs together; and on stage, their distinctive harmonization was a visual and musical embodiment of their rapport. Producer George Martin was initially reluctant to record Lennon & McCartney-penned material but is said to have changed his mind when he heard "Please Please Me". Written entirely by John in his bedroom at his Aunt Mimi's house, it was his attempt to imitate Roy Orbison's falsetto style.

Bottom left: A very lucky nine-year-old, Anne Escreet, enjoys the photo opportunity of a lifetime when she has the attention of all four band members after a concert in Hull. The Beatles had played in the town twice before but this was their first show at the ABC Cinema in November 1963.

Opposite: John plays acoustic guitar when he and the rest of the Fab Four appear on *The Ken Dodd Show* in November 1963. They performed the two songs from their soon-to-be-released single – "I Want to Hold Your Hand" and the B-side, "This Boy"; both were mimed.

"Touring was a relief, just to get out of Liverpool and break new ground. We were beginning to feel stale and cramped. We'd outlived the Hamburg stage and wanted to pack that up. We hated going back to Hamburg those last two times. We'd had all that scene."
—John

I just like records...

Left: 1963 continued as a never-ending round of major gigs – mostly in large-town ballrooms or theatres – and small club venues. John became increasingly disinterested in live performances – the noise from the frenzied fans, who would scream through most numbers, meant he was often not able to hear the music and himself singing. "I'm a record man. I just like records", he is reported to have commented. It would be another three years before the band's last live concert.

Below: The Beatles try to make their escape from fans on the night of their appearance at the London Palladium. *Sunday Night at the London Palladium* in October 1963 was a big breakthrough for the band. The variety entertainment show regularly drew audiences of up to 15 million and gave The Beatles the national exposure Brian was working for. They topped the bill, closing the show with "Twist and Shout", but not before John, with characteristic acerbity, had told the younger, screaming fans who were in the audience to "Shut up". John didn't dislike the fans but his temperament was not one of patience and he didn't like the demands of celebrity.

Opposite middle: Brian's styling of the band and the carefully posed publicity shots helped to counter their reputation for being long-haired and rebellious. But John was not afraid to speak as he felt; as the most outspoken of The Beatles, he quickly became the band member most sought after for interviews. He was articulate, interesting and not afraid to move away from the predictable questions and onto politics and religion.

> "For our last number I'd like to ask your help. Would the people in the cheaper seats, clap your hands. And the rest of you, if you'll just rattle your jewellery." — **John**

Above left: The sight of crazed fans at the Winter Garden Theatre, Bournemouth, was captured by an American journalist, who broadcast the scenes on US television.

Above right: The boys take a break in the empty stalls of a London theatre ahead of a performance. Brian Epstein was soon to insist that they no longer played in the ballrooms, preferring instead venues with fixed seating where access to the band by the often hysterical audience was more controllable.

Below left and right: With his outspoken views and often edgy personality, John knew how to entertain people and was often the centre of attention after concerts. He would later express anger over meeting dignitaries and signing autographs for policeman and promoters – but he was conscientious in setting aside time for the true fans, particularly in the early days.

> With his outspoken views and often edgy personality, John knew how to entertain people and was often the centre of attention after concerts.

JOHN LENNON TIMELINE

1963

11 Jan Release of "Please Please Me".

19 Jan The Beatles make their national television debut, on *Thank Your Lucky Stars*.

11 Feb The Beatles record their first album in one eleven-hour session.

22 Feb Formation of Northern Songs; publishers of all future Lennon-McCartney songs.

2 Mar "Please Please Me" is at the top of the *Melody Maker* chart, and at the number one position on at least two other charts. The album of the same name is to go to number one later in the month.

8 Apr John becomes a father as Cynthia gives birth to a son, John Charles Julian Lennon.

11 Apr Release of "From Me To You", The Beatles' third single. It is to be the first of eleven consecutive single releases to top the British chart, through to 1966.

28 Apr John goes on holiday to Spain with Brian Epstein.

21 Jun The *Daily Mirror* reports that John Lennon had beaten up Cavern Club DJ, Bob Wooler, on 18 June, at Paul's twenty-first birthday party. Apparently Wooler was hospitalized after suggesting that Lennon was having an affair with Epstein.

29 Jun John's first solo television appearance on BBC's *Juke Box Jury*.

3 Aug The Beatles perform for the last time at the Cavern Club.

23 Aug UK single release of "She Loves You"/ "I'll Get You".

4 Nov John utters his celebrated "...rattle your jewellery" witticism at The Royal Variety Performance, Prince of Wales Theatre, London.

29 Nov UK single release of "I Want To Hold Your Hand"/ "This Boy".

27 Dec John and Paul are described as "the outstanding English composers of 1963" in *The Times*.

By the end of 1963, The Beatles had played over 160 concerts at venues throughout the country.

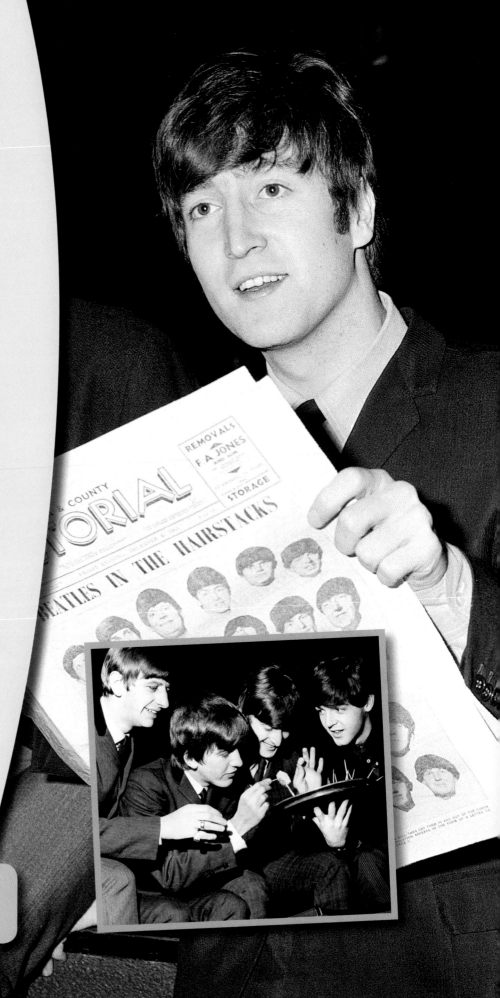

The demands of Beatlemania

Opposite inset: In an image typical of the band's playfulness, Paul offers his bandmates cheese on cocktail sticks at a reception celebrating their forthcoming UK tour. Their first major British tour, supporting the 16-year-old Helen Shapiro, coincided with the release of their second single, "Please Please Me", in the spring of 1963. They were fourth on the bill of an eleven-act line up. Shapiro remembers having an enormous crush on John, six years her senior; he was very protective of her, making sure she ate properly when they were travelling between gigs.

Middle right: In south London the queue for tickets had grown overnight despite the rain. Although Beatlemania did not sweep through Britain until the autumn of 1963, there were early signs of it during the tour; the boys were making the news and the adulation of the fans was on the rise (opposite main image). Queueing for tickets became a matter of controlling the crowds. By the end of the year, they had covered most of the country in four major tours, punctuated by a short trip to Sweden at the end of October. They shared the bill with Helen Shapiro, Tommy Roe and Chris Montez, eventually topping it with Roy Orbison and Gerry and the Pacemakers.

Top right: The band take a break but look too tired to even drink their tea during their autumn tour. In November 1963, they managed only four nights off and at the end of the year they had played over 160 concerts at venues throughout the country.

Below right: Again the boys look exhausted as they sit down to sign a series of autograph books between shows.

Below left: Their new-found fame meant that the band were in demand everywhere; they used it to support good causes, such as the Oxfam Hunger £Million Campaign. This image was used on a promotional card sent to people who raised money for the cause.

Christmas Eve '63

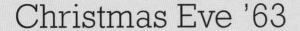

Opposite top: The autumn tour – the fourth of the year – began with The Beatles as undisputed headliners. They were supported by, among others, The Vernon Girls, a group of female singers originally formed by the Vernons Pools Company in Liverpool. In 1963 they were recording covers of US hits but the following year they charted with "We Love the Beatles", which contained the line: "Now Johnny is the leader..."

Opposite bottom: At Christmas The Beatles took the prestigious guest spot on the *Morecambe and Wise Show*, where they joined the legendary British comedy duo in several sketches as well as performing three numbers, including "I Want to Hold Your Hand". In boating attire, they give a rendition of an old classic, "On Moonlight Bay", to close the show.

Top right: The boys in costume for their first Christmas show at the Finsbury Park Astoria on Christmas Eve 1963. The repertoire of six songs – including "I Want to Hold Your Hand", "Roll Over Beethoven" and "Twist and Shout" – was interspersed with support acts and playful skits and gave the show a feeling of pantomime.

Below: At every gig both the local and national press were keen to photograph the band. By the end of 1963, Brian had secured a series of dates in Paris, a planned tour of Australia and New Zealand and successfully negotiated three appearances on *The Ed Sullivan Show* in the US. Stardom had well and truly arrived and they were on the brink of conquering America.

CHAPTER TWO

1964

You know I feel alright

In 1964, after consolidating their phenomenal success in Britain, The Beatles were ready to conquer America. No other popular British group had made it big in the States, but John, Paul, George and Ringo were ready to change all that. Their records were already climbing the US charts in February, and soon afterwards the group arrived to appear on *The Ed Sullivan Show* and to give concerts at the Washington Coliseum and Carnegie Hall. Their reception at John F. Kennedy Airport was wildly enthusiastic, as America succumbed to The Beatles in typically wholehearted fashion.

As well as visiting New York and Washington, the boys also spent a few days in Miami, where they not only appeared again live on *The Ed Sullivan Show* and taped a third performance to be shown later, but also managed a few days of rest and relaxation. Wherever they went, the now-familiar scenes of pandemonium unfolded yet again as American fans went crazy. They also met up with boxer Cassius Clay, who was in Miami preparing to fight Sonny Liston for the World Heavyweight Title. Predictably John pushed his luck with a smart remark to the champ, but luckily Clay saw the joke.

After their brief visit to America, the group returned home to begin work on their first film, *A Hard Day's Night*, at Twickenham Studios. The storyline was based on incidents from their own lives, a kind of fictionalized documentary of the crazy lives of the world's most famous pop stars. The concept had come from a comment John had made, about how little they had seen of the country during a recent tour

of Sweden. Many scenes were shot on location, which was a major logistical exercise, since the fans would quickly gather in their hundreds. For many weeks the film had only a working title, but after Ringo talked of "a hard day's night" when recalling a heavy night, everyone realized it was the perfect phrase. The title song, another Lennon-McCartney composition, was sung by John. Although it was made in black and white, the film was an instant success with the fans and the soundtrack LP quickly went to the top of the UK charts.

Apart from his song-writing, in his spare time John wrote poems and prose, or doodled. He had already had several articles published and had also written a column under the name Beatcomber in the Liverpool newspaper, *Mersey Beat*. In March 1964 some of his work was published by Jonathan Cape in a book entitled *In His Own Write*. It not only received very complimentary reviews, it also topped the bestseller list in Britain, and in April a Foyle's literary luncheon was held in his honour at the Dorchester Hotel in London. Despite the tradition that the guest of honour should make a substantial speech, John's lasted precisely five seconds. Many guests were disappointed, but he said later that he was scared stiff and did not feel up to speaking for longer.

After four weeks off in May, the longest rest The Beatles had managed for some considerable time, they were ready to begin their first world tour. They were to play thirty-two concerts in nineteen days, across Europe, Australia and New Zealand. The day before their departure disaster struck when Ringo collapsed during a photo-shoot and was rushed to hospital suffering from tonsillitis and pharyngitis. The tour still had to go ahead, so he was quickly replaced by Jimmy Nicol, an experienced session drummer, for the first few dates. Luckily Ringo was well enough to join the

Left: John chats to Mary Wilson, wife of the future British Prime Minister, Harold Wilson, at the Variety Club Awards ceremony at the Dorchester Hotel in March 1964. The Beatles were presented with The Show Business Personalities of 1963 Award.

tour in Melbourne, and stayed for the rest of the run. Two weeks before they were due to leave, John had phoned his Aunt Mimi and invited her along too, and in New Zealand she made sure he took some time out to visit relatives. John had never met them before, as they had emigrated from Liverpool years earlier to become farmers.

Beatlemania now followed the band wherever they appeared – and not just at concert venues. Whenever the plane stopped for refuelling, even in the middle of the night in the remotest of places, crowds of screaming fans would appear from nowhere. Although at first the fame and attention had been flattering, it had quickly gone beyond a joke. It had become a major logistical exercise to get the band to and from the venue in safety, and once inside they had to stay cooped up in their dressing rooms, prisoners of their own fame. On stage, they had to dodge around to avoid being hit by the gifts and sweets being thrown by fans and the screaming completely drowned out the sound of the music. John perhaps resented this the most, and was already beginning to regard the live concerts as pointless, since the fans' reaction obviously had little to do with the music. On stage he now often did not bother to sing, just opened and closed his mouth, because he reasoned that no-one could have heard him anyway. Concert tours had become a mind-numbing routine of arriving in town, being smuggled into a venue, performing a show, being hustled into a van for a high-speed getaway to a nearby hotel, and then holing up overnight until it was time to go through it all again the next day. John and the others could not go out in public without being mobbed, their homes were under constant siege from fans and anything not securely fixed down was instantly stolen as a memento.

In July the world charity premiere at the London Pavilion of *A Hard Day's Night*, attended by all four Beatles, caused scenes of chaos in central London. John disliked crowds – he told several journalists that he felt uncomfortable surrounded by many people. Since he was so short-sighted, and had great trouble with the contact lenses he now wore, he was often unaware of just how many people were around.

A second showing of the film in Liverpool was followed by a civic reception held for the group in Liverpool Town Hall – a mark of how successful The Beatles had become. Thousands of people turned out on the day, but John was surprised to find that his old home, Mendips, had become a shrine visited by fans and journalists from around the world. Mimi still lived there alone, but she seemed to take the constant intrusions in her stride. She worried about the fans, and sometimes invited them in for a cup of tea if they looked hungry or cold.

Although John was already a millionaire, he and Cynthia still had no house of their own. At first Cynthia and Julian had deliberately been kept in the background – mainly at Brian Epstein's instigation, as he felt that if the fans knew John was married with a child they would lose interest. However, the secret inevitably got out and it seemed to make very little difference. Their flat in west London was constantly surrounded by fans, so in August 1965 John bought Kenwood, a mansion on an estate in Weybridge, which offered more privacy. Since money was no object, he had the whole place decorated, installed an expensive swimming pool and had various other changes made – he ended up spending almost twice what he had paid for the house itself. George and Ringo both lived nearby, but Paul stayed in central London, later buying a house in St John's Wood.

After a few bookings in Britain and another short tour to Sweden, in August The Beatles set off on their first full American tour. It consisted of thirty-two shows in twenty-four cities within thirty-four days so John and the others spent almost the entire time travelling. Again they saw very little of the places they visited, only crowds of rampaging fans wherever they went. However, one important event during the tour was a meeting with Bob Dylan. John admired the American singer's work, and he wrote several songs in the Dylan style. Despite this the two men were too close temperamentally to become great friends although John did later invite Dylan to his home in Weybridge. Dylan is also popularly supposed to have introduced The Beatles to marijuana. In Hamburg they had experimented with booze and Preludin – a pep pill – but John soon took to marijuana with great enthusiasm.

When The Beatles returned to Britain from America, to the usual hysterical scenes at London Airport, the Prime Minister, Sir Alec Douglas-Home, called them "our best exports" and "a useful contribution to the balance of payments". Only four years previously, John had been a penniless art student; now he was a millionaire, a world-famous pop star, known and sought after by debutantes, dowagers, lords and leading politicians. However, like the other Beatles, he hated being paraded around in front of dignitaries and even more he hated the thought that what had started out as rock 'n' roll was now an industry. As he told a fellow musician at the time, it felt uncomfortably as if he had sold his soul to the devil.

Opposite: John and the rest of the band are introduced to Princess Margaret at the premiere of *A Hard Day's Night*.

"Mersey beaucoup"

Top left: John and George leave London Airport for a three-week stint at the Olympia Theatre in Paris in January 1964. The band's cool and relatively small reception at Le Bourget Airport was in contrast to those in the UK, where screaming fans would greet them wherever they went. The French audiences seemed indifferent to The Beatles' performances; at one concert, with quick wit and humour, John replied to the half-hearted applause with "Mersey beaucoup".

Top middle: John sips a cup of tea at London Airport on his way back to France. He returned to London a couple of times to discuss the band's stint in Paris with Brian Epstein. Despite the lukewarm reception there, good news had arrived – the band's single, "I Want To Hold Your Hand", had become their first number one in the US.

Top right and bottom left: Returning with the rest of The Beatles from the Paris commitment, John sports a leather Breton cap, which he seemed particularly fond of wearing.

Left middle: John and the rest of the band face an American journalist ahead of their first trip to the States. While they were still in Paris, Capitol Records had released *Meet the Beatles!* for the US market with the strapline "The first album by England's phenomenal pop combo". It reached the top of the album charts and went on to sell over 5 million copies.

Cynthia Lennon

Save for the loss of her father when she was seventeen, Cynthia Powell enjoyed a comfortable middle-class upbringing in a pleasant Liverpool suburb. She showed an artistic bent from an early age, and at eighteen enrolled at Liverpool College of Art, where she was both intimidated and drawn by the disruptive, acerbic Teddy Boy with whom she shared a lettering class. The magnetism won out when John made his play for the shy, bespectacled Cynthia in the summer of 1958. They quickly became inseparable lovers, Cynthia moulding her appearance to accord with John's blonde bombshell fantasy, Brigitte Bardot. Cynthia was pregnant when they married on 23 August 1962, John Charles Julian arriving on 8 April the following year. As Beatlemania swept the country, Cynthia was consigned to the background as it was deemed bad for business for a pop star to have a wife and child in tow. In the early years of their marriage, she and Julian saw little of John, who was either on tour or in the recording studio – and when he was at home, his lifestyle did not always fit with the routines of family life. The marriage was soon in trouble, and according to Cynthia it was John's drug habit that caused the rot to set in, long before Yoko Ono's arrival on the scene. "We were on different mental planes," she reflected, and the divisions were highlighted when John met the avant-garde artist who was very much on his wavelength. The Lennons divorced in November 1968, with Yoko cited in the proceedings. Cynthia subsequently married three times: Italian hotelier Roberto Bassanini (1970–73); Lancastrian engineer John Twist (1976–83); and nightclub owner Noel Charles (2002– until his death in 2013). Cynthia died in 2015.

By the time The Beatles set out to conquer America, the press had discovered that John was married and Cynthia was thrust into the limelight.

Above: John and Cynthia wait to board the plane to the US at the start of the band's first trip to the States in February 1964. The pair had been married for 18 months by this point. A married Beatle – and a father to boot – was not deemed good publicity and Epstein persuaded John to keep his family life secret. However, by the time The Beatles set out to conquer America, the press had unearthed the truth and Cynthia was thrust into the limelight. As the band left London Airport, John agreed to being photographed with her by his side; in contrast in New York, Cynthia was left behind as the boys were taken around the city by car.

America welcomes The Beatles

Top right: Arriving at John F Kennedy Airport, New York, the band step off the plane to be greeted by 3,000 screaming fans. The chaotic scenes would have put to bed any lingering doubts about their ability to conquer the States. Shrieking fans threw jelly beans and candy kisses; hundreds of policemen struggled to keep back the fans as reporters, cameramen and photographers clamoured for The Beatles' attention.

Middle right: John shares the reins with Ringo as they and Paul take a ride in Central Park the day after arriving in New York. Back at the hotel, George had stayed in bed suffering from a sore throat.

Below: The Beatles playing live on *The Ed Sullivan Show*. Over 70 million people tuned in to see them perform five songs. As the camera lingered on John, the caption "Sorry girls, he's married" was shown on the screen.

Opposite middle: Bad weather meant the boys had to take the train, rather than the plane, from New York to Washington DC. Despite this, they find time to pose for the cameras in a mock snowball fight.

Opposite: The cold weather meant fewer fans and less frenzied scenes, which allowed John and the rest of the group more freedom to move around the capital. They were able to sightsee – the White House was one of their stops – with relative ease, accompanied by just a handful of press photographers.

> On 9 February over 70 million people tuned in to see the Fab Four perform five songs on *The Ed Sullivan Show*.

"The Beatles appear to be a harmless, youthful, fad; like rolling hula hoops and swallowing goldfish". *New York World Telegram* review of the *Ed Sullivan Show*

Beatlemania hits Washington

Above left: John, Paul, Ringo and George at the Plaza Hotel in New York. The city police patrolled the hotel lobby and the corridor outside their 12th-floor rooms as hundreds of fans stood behind barriers outside the hotel. Inside, John and the rest of the band were busy taking calls from journalists and DJs; Epstein put a stop to the "free" interviews as soon as he found out.

Top right and middle: Performing to an audience of around 20,000, The Beatles play their first US concert at the Washington Coliseum on 11 February 1964. Playing on a stage in the centre of the auditorium proved a new challenge for the boys, who had to reposition themselves at intervals to allow the whole audience a good view. John's casual remark in an earlier interview about George's favourite sweet being jelly babies, led to the fans throwing jelly beans (the US nearest equivalent) throughout the show. The atmosphere at the concert, which was the biggest they had ever played, certainly fired up the band; but the enthusiasm proved relatively short-lived. John in particular, came to hate the huge impersonal venues where they could not hear themselves perform above the screaming hysteria of the fans.

Bottom right: With Brian Epstein standing behind him, John waves to photographers at a publicity event at the British Embassy in Washington after the Coliseum concert. The event turned sour when a guest cut a lock of Ringo's hair without his permission. Lennon was furious and later complained that "wherever we went we were supposed to not be normal" and were "touched and pawed". The boys left in the middle of the reception in disgust.

Opposite: The Beatles in Washington DC. Their sightseeing itinerary doubled as a photo opportunity for the American press. John and the boys were accompanied by David and Albert Maysles, an American film-making team, who documented this first visit.

John in particular, came to hate the huge impersonal venues where they could not hear themselves perform above the screaming hysteria of the fans.

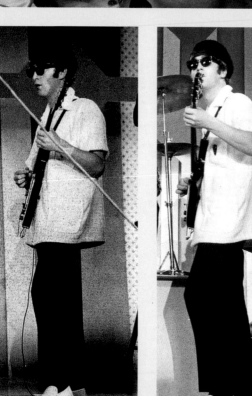

Welcome to Florida

Above, left and below: After the Coliseum gig the Beatles made a brief return to New York, where they performed two short sets at Carnegie Hall. John had nothing positive to say about the venue, bemoaning the fact that the acoustics were terrible. He later described it as a circus for the rich and famous with the band being presented like animals in cages. They flew to Florida the next day and never played Carnegie again. The warmer climes of Florida, and more specifically Miami Beach, was the location for the band's second appearance on *The Ed Sullivan Show*. Despite their tight schedule, they managed to take some time out. Cruising on a luxury yacht, *The Southern Trail*, the boys were able to relax, take their own photographs and soak up the sun.

Bottom left: John rehearses at the Deauville Hotel, where The Beatles were staying, ahead of the group's performance on *The Ed Sullivan Show* the following day. The 2600-strong audience for the recording watched the band perform six songs, including "I Want to Hold Your Hand" and "She Loves You". The show reached 70 million people across the US. A third show, also recorded in Miami, aired after the boys had returned to England. The Beatles had well and truly arrived.

Opposite: John takes a break from the rock.'n' roll lifestyle and downs a pint of milk.

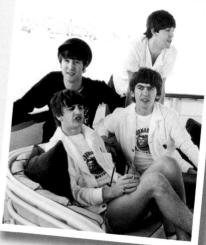

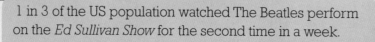

1 in 3 of the US population watched The Beatles perform on the *Ed Sullivan Show* for the second time in a week.

"Wish they'd invent pills. Eating wastes a part of your life. I like tea and cornflakes and that." —John

Making waves in Miami

Wherever they went they were followed by photographers and onlookers, who at this point kept their distance so the band were still able to enjoy Miami Beach. John described Miami as "... Blackpool... with palm trees – and mink".

As John and the boys appeared to revel in the attention, Cynthia, who had accompanied John on the trip, remained firmly in the background. In an interview for the *Daily Mail* on the beach in Miami, she was portrayed as "...the wife who doesn't exist". Happy enough not to be in the limelight, she nevertheless commented that the high price of fame was a loss of personal freedom.

At the beginning of February, shortly before the the boys arrived in New York, "I Want to Hold Your Hand" became the Beatles' first No. 1 in the *Billboard* Hot 100. "She Loves You" followed suit in March and by the time they made their next trip to the United States in August, it would be dangerous to leave the hotel room without protection.

JOHN LENNON TIMELINE

1964

Jan The Beatles embark on a low-key French tour. They are informed by a telegram from Capitol Records in New York of their first US number-one single, "I Want To Hold Your Hand".

9 Feb The Beatles perform on *The Ed Sullivan Show* in the US.

11 Feb The Beatles play their first concert in the US, at the Washington Coliseum.

2 Mar The Beatles begin shooting their first film, *A Hard Day's Night*.

20 Mar UK single release of "Can't Buy Me Love"/ "You Can't Do That".

23 Mar The Beatles are presented Carl-Alan awards by The Duke of Edinburgh.

23 Mar *In His Own Write*, John's first book, is published. The first print-run quickly sells out.

4 Apr The Beatles occupy the top five positions of the American singles chart.

23 Apr John attends a Foyle's literary luncheon, held in his honour. He declines to make a much-hoped-for speech.

6 Jul The Beatles' film *A Hard Day's Night* premieres in London.

10 Jul UK single release of "A Hard Day's Night"/ "Things We Said Today".

10 Jul A civic reception is held in Liverpool to honour The Beatles.

15 Jul John buys a mansion, Kenwood, in Weybridge, Surrey.

18 Aug The Beatles leave London for their first major US tour.

28 Aug The Beatles are introduced to Bob Dylan, who in turn introduces them to marijuana.

27 Nov UK single release of "I Feel Fine"/ "She's A Woman".

"
''It's Blackpool – with palm trees – and mink''
—John describing Miami

Who's the greatest?

Opposite and above: John pushes his luck with "the greatest": While in Miami, The Beatles meet Cassius Clay before his world heavyweight title fight with Sonny Liston. Liston, the favourite, had been in the audience at the second *The Ed Sullivan Show* and initially it was hoped they would meet him and "...not the loudmouth who's going to lose", as John so eloquently put it. Clay was a second-best but it turned out that the boys had picked a winner when he went on to defeat Liston. The world's top group were instantly allied with "the greatest".

Right: After a visit lasting little more than two weeks and stopping in only three cities, The Beatles flew back from the US to Britain on 22 February. Arriving at London Airport, they were greeted by crowds of screaming fans.

> "They keep telling me I'm all right for money but then I think I may have spent it all by the time I'm 40, so I keep going"
> —John talking to Maureen Cleave, *Daily Mail*

Making a movie

Opposite: John and Paul on set having their hair styled during the filming of *A Hard Day's Night*, which began on 2 March 1964. John later described acting as "daft" and he remembered how nervous they had all been during their first days on set filming aboard a train at Paddington Station, saying: "Practically the whole train bit we were going to pieces".

Work on the soundtrack album was already underway before filming commenced and continued at Abbey Road until June.

A Hard Day's Night is the only Beatles' album on which all the songs were written by Lennon and McCartney although John worked alone on many of the tracks, including the title track and the beautiful ballad, "If I Fell". The film received two Oscar nominations, one for the screenplay and the other for the score.

Above: At the Variety Club of Great Britain annual awards ceremony at the Dorchester Hotel in London, John accepts his Silver Heart award. He could not resist injecting some risqué humour by thanking the Club for their "Purple Hearts" – a well-known amphetamine of the day.

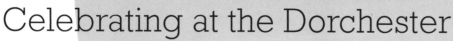

Celebrating at the Dorchester

Opposite below right: Harold Wilson, then Leader of the Labour Opposition, recognized there were votes to be had by being "with it". A northerner with a Liverpool constituency, Wilson had previously referred to The Beatles as the Conservative's "secret weapon". In a bullish attempt to align himself with the Four, he arranged to host the Variety Club annual awards in March 1964. Wilson went on to win the 1964 General Election; The Beatles had declined to vote at all.

Above: John chats with Brian Epstein at the Dorchester and (below right) actor Patrick MacNee approaches Paul and John.

Above centre: Thumbs up at the awards ceremony. By this time, John and the boys were feeling the strain of their exhausting schedule. Their US visit had been followed by recording sessions, interviews and appearances; and the filming schedule for *A Hard Day's Night* was relentless throughout March and April. Immediately after the Variety lunch, they headed for the BBC Television Theatre in Shepherd's Bush, west London, to record their debut appearance on *Top of the Pops*.

Pop and Politics

Below: John sips coffee with Mary Wilson at the Variety Club luncheon. Despite the fact that he was often ill at ease mixing with dignitaries on such occasions, he seemed perfectly relaxed with the future PM's wife.

Opposite: A day after their debut on *Top of the Pops* John mimes to "Can't Buy Me Love" on the band's second appearance on ITV's *Ready Steady Go!*

"Azue orl gnome, Harrassed Wilsod won the General Erection with a very small marjorie over the Torchies"
From *A Spaniard in the Works*

John: In His Own Write

Left: The Beatles pose with Walter Shenson, producer of *A Hard Day's Night*. John took the opportunity to publicize his book, *In His Own Write*, published at the end of March.

Below left and right: On the same day as the publication of *In His Own Write*, the band are presented to the Duke of Edinburgh at the Carl-Alan Awards in London. They received two awards: Best Group of 1963 and Best Vocal Record for "She Loves You". Despite outward appearances, John was becoming disenchanted with their courtship by "the elite"; he once said, "I'm sick of meeting people I don't want to meet. Boring lord mayors and all that...They keep sending in autograph books and we sign them only to find that they belong to officials, promoters, police and all that lot".

Opposite top left: A thoughtful John caught unawares on camera.

Opposite below right and left: A literary lunch was held at the Dorchester Hotel to celebrate the publication of *In His Own Write*. John had been writing amusing stories and poems since childhood; the book was really a continuation of *The Daily Howl* – a collection of doodles and nonsense verse he had produced while at Quarry Bank High School. His love of and talent for wordplay mixed with absurdist humour was evident. This debut publication had received some critical acclaim, with the first edition being an immediate sell-out. Those assembled at the lunch were less impressed with the guest of honour, whose brief contribution to the proceedings of "Thank you all very much; you've got a lucky face", left them non-plussed.

Opposite top right: John chats to Lionel Bart, composer of the musical *Oliver!*, at the Dorchester event.

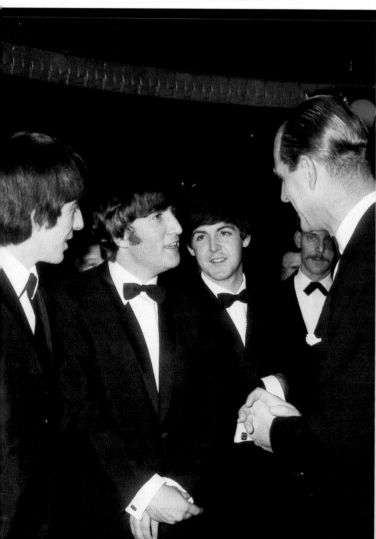

"A 'remarkable' book which was worth the attention of anyone who fears for the impoverishment of the English language and British imagination".
Times Literary Supplement review of *In His Own Write*

Suited for the Scala

Right: After filming the concert performance sequence for *A Hard Day's Night* at the Scala Theatre, London, The Beatles returned to the venue to shoot more scenes. Here, the boys help John with the sleeve of his jacket.

Above: John demonstrates a dance routine to George and three young women while filming *A Hard Day's Night*.

Below left: John is measured for a new suit. The Beatles' image of smart mohair suits, white shirts, dark ties and a tight-fitting Cuban-heeled boot – called the "Beatle boot" – was prescribed by Brian Epstein at the beginning of his relationship with the band. John would often add to this image with a Breton cap. Some commented that "his wardrobe was as sharp as his wit".

Right inset: At this time John's father, Fred, had reappeared in the singer's life after a 19-year absence. He turned up, with a journalist in tow, at the offices of NEMS Enterprises. John met with him after filming and, at Brian Epstein's suggestion, Fred Lennon was given a modest weekly allowance. Relations between him and John were at best neutral and became hostile when Fred tried to cash in on his son's success by releasing a record, "That's My Life".

John's father, Fred, had reappeared in the singer's life after a 19-year absence. He turned up, with a journalist in tow, at the offices of NEMS Enterprises.

Above: John and George take a break on set from filming *A Hard Day's Night*. There was much down-time while making the movie and at one point a dispute over unpaid extras brought the film to a standstill. The extras, among whom was a young Phil Collins, were given a nominal fee and a free lunch.

Celebrated author

Opposite and inset: John and Cynthia arrive for the Foyles literary lunch to mark the publication of *In His Own Write*. The pair had been out the night before with the rest of The Beatles to celebrate the book's success and it seemed that John's lacklustre and very short speech as the guest of honour was the result of feeling the worse for wear.

Below: The boys visit Madame Tussauds to be photographed alongside their waxwork effigies. They were the first pop group to appear in the Museum and over the years the figures had to be reworked as the band's image changed. The waxworks were used by Peter Blake and Jann Haworth on the iconic *Sgt Pepper* album cover three years later. In 1966 an exhausted John, disenchanted with performing live, remarked, "...we could send out four wax dummies of ourselves and that would satisfy the crowds."

Far right: John dressed as a trumpeter in heraldic costume for their television special *Around The Beatles*.

The first edition of *In His Own Write* sold out immediately, the public eager to see where the "witty" Beatle's flights of fancy had taken him.

Touring Scotland

Right and Far right: After the Madame Tussauds photo opportunity, The Beatles set off on a mini-tour of Scotland. John and the boys arrive at Turnhouse Airport in Edinburgh on 29 April to a warm, if blustery, reception from their fans.

Below: Scotland lays out the welcome mat. Booked to play sell-out shows in both the Scottish capital and Glasgow over consecutive nights, they headed to the ABC cinema in Edinburgh where they pose for press photographs before performing two evening sets. The following day they put on two shows at the Glasgow Odeon.

The Scottish mini-tour proved so popular that the band returned in October for gigs in Edinburgh, Glasgow and Dundee.

This page: More publicity shots and the opportunity for some lucky fan to meet his idols. The limited capacity of cinemas, used as regular concert venues, meant that large numbers of fans who wanted to see the shows were disappointed. The short tour proved so popular that the band returned in October for more gigs in Edinburgh and Glasgow, adding Dundee to their itinerary.

With his young fans

This page: John looks relaxed as he poses for pictures with a young fan. John valued his genuine fans, especially the younger ones, and took time to sign autographs and chat to the young people who came to see the band.

John was a regular visitor to Scotland during his childhood. While he was living with his Aunt Mimi, another of his mother's sisters Aunt Mater (Elizabeth) moved to Edinburgh and John regularly travelled from Liverpool to stay with the family in Ormidale Terrace, near Murrayfield Stadium, during the summer holidays. After spending time in the city, he often accompanied them on trips to the Highlands, where they stayed in a cottage at Durness in Sutherland. There John enjoyed a lifestyle far removed from that in his Liverpool suburb.

Opposite: John was prepared to do what was necessary to be "bigger than Elvis" but had already begun to realize that such a life was not genuinely fulfilling.

> John valued his genuine fans, especially the younger ones and took time to sign autographs and chat to the young people who came to see them.

Meeting and greeting

Above, right and opposite top: John generally viewed authority figures with suspicion but here he seems happy to enjoy a drink backstage with the Lord Provost of Edinburgh, even taking the time to inspect the Provost's chain of office. In general though, he and the others turned down invitations to official functions, where they felt they were regarded as freaks by the other guests. On this occasion, the relaxed mood was slightly marred when the Lord Provost asked The Beatles if they would make a large donation to help fund the Edinburgh Festival – they suggested that he pawn the chain to resolve the problem.

Opposite below: The demands of fame on John's daily life were certainly considerable but by mid-1964 record sales and song-writing royalties had made him a millionaire. Despite this, he still had time for the genuine fans and enjoyed meeting them up close.

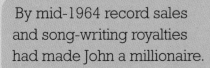
By mid-1964 record sales and song-writing royalties had made John a millionaire.

On stage in Edinburgh

Above: John on stage at the Edinburgh gig. The noise of the screaming fans was so loud, most of the time it was impossible for anyone to hear the music. John would often finish the song with an obscenity – as a form of release from the tension – but the fans never heard it.

Right: For the camera, John jokes about the way to the stage at the ABC cinema. The punishing schedule meant that eventually the band would scarcely know which town they were in, let alone which theatre.

Opposite: John signs an autograph before going on stage at the ABC cinema in Edinburgh.

John plays a dream role

Right: Recorded for ITV and broadcast in May 1964, *Around The Beatles* consisted of musical performances by the band and guests. A spoof of the "play within a play" from Shakespeare's *A Midsummer Night's Dream*, in which John took the female role of Thisbe, also featured. Here, in costume, he tends to Paul McCartney's Pyramus.

Below right and opposite: A break in the hectic schedule in May allowed The Beatles some time for rest and relaxation. John and Cynthia, along with George and Pattie, flew to Hawaii under assumed names in an attempt to elude the press but they were rumbled and photographers and journalists were there to "greet" them when they landed in Honolulu. Seeking privacy, they travelled on to the remote island of Tahiti, where John was able to write *A Spaniard in the Works*. The Lennons returned to Britain at the end of May.

Below: Back from their break, the band reunite at the Prince of Wales Theatre for two concerts and a press conference, days before the start of the world tour in June.

Preparing for the World tour

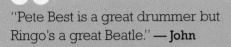

"Pete Best is a great drummer but Ringo's a great Beatle." — **John**

Main image: John looks thoughtful before going on stage at the Prince of Wales Theatre. The Beatles topped the bill and performed seven songs that evening. Free bars became a normal feature of the band's lives, and as their fame and wealth increased, so too did their drinking, especially John's, whose arguments would sometimes become more emotional after a few too many Scotch and Cokes.

Below inset: John warms up before the Prince of Wales concert, while Ringo relaxes behind his drum kit with a cigarette.

Opposite: In Leeds John helps himself to a drink and Paul provides the ice.

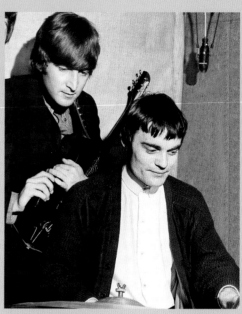

John introduces Jimmy

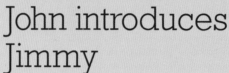

Above right and right: Jimmy Nicol rehearses with John and Paul. On the eve of their world tour, Ringo was taken ill with tonsillitis and rushed to hospital. John and the boys felt that the start of the tour would have to be cancelled but with tickets sold and fans to satisfy, Epstein decided they must honour the contract. Jimmy Nicol – an accomplished session drummer who looked the part – was familiar with The Beatles' material and was known to George Martin. He was drafted in for the first leg of the tour in Denmark, Holland, Hong Kong and two dates in Australia. Ringo flew out and rejoined the band on 14 June.

Top left, left and below right: John and Jimmy share a joke and greet the crowds in Adelaide as they arrive in Australia. The band's reception there was phenomenal, even by Beatle standards – several attendance records were broken at their concerts, crowds gathered at the airports and lined the six-mile route to the city centre, while around 300,000 massed in the streets outside their Adelaide hotel.

Above middle: Looking down from their hotel balcony in Sydney, John jokes with the crowd.

> Nicol said he felt like an interloper in "the most exclusive club in the world".

The band would never return to Australia and the fans milked it for every last moment.

Above: John and Cynthia move quickly to escape the crowds as The Beatles arrive back in Britain from Australia at the end of their world tour. Cynthia was, by now, used to dodging the fans and photographers; but for John's Aunt Mimi, whom he had flown out to New Zealand for the last leg of the tour, experiencing "Beatlemania" first-hand must have been a shock.

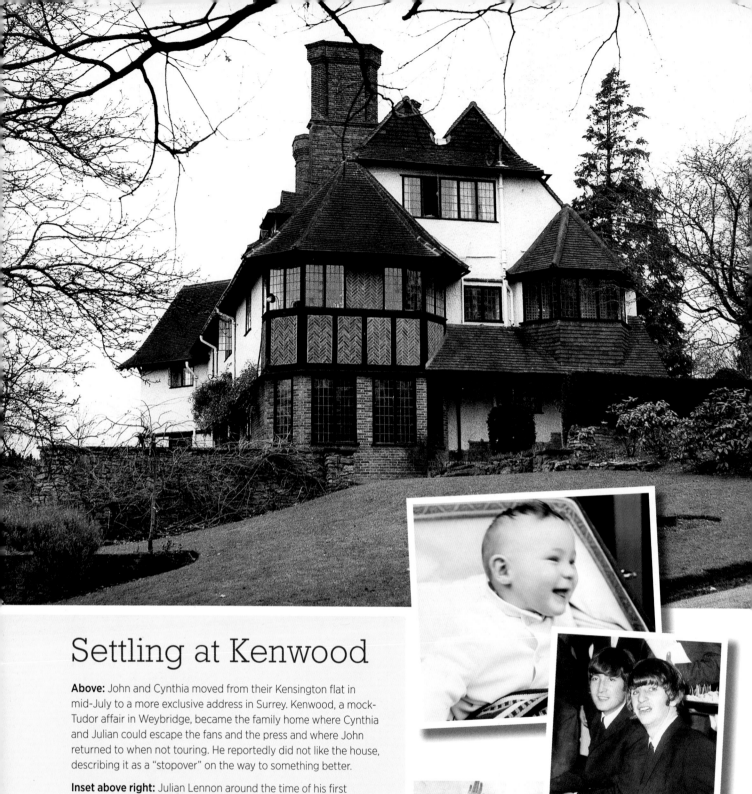

Settling at Kenwood

Above: John and Cynthia moved from their Kensington flat in mid-July to a more exclusive address in Surrey. Kenwood, a mock-Tudor affair in Weybridge, became the family home where Cynthia and Julian could escape the fans and the press and where John returned to when not touring. He reportedly did not like the house, describing it as a "stopover" on the way to something better.

Inset above right: Julian Lennon around the time of his first birthday. When the British press realized John was married with a child, they snapped pictures of Julian despite Cynthia claiming to be her own twin sister in a desperate, if improbable, plan to elude them.

Bottom right: When the boys returned from Australia in July, the crowds that greeted them were larger than those in February when they had returned from the States.

Middle right: John and Ringo attend a civic reception in Liverpool held to celebrate the premiere of *A Hard Day's Night*, that evening. The return to their home town gave John the chance to catch up with some of his family.

> "John Lennon will take along his Aunt Mimi on their Australia tour. Mrs Mimi Smith said last night 'John gave me no excuse for turning the trip down. He's a pet for giving me such a treat. I've never travelled so far from home before.'"
> — Extracted from the *Daily Mail* 27 May 1964

Above: Although Cynthia accompanied John to premieres and galas in London, she did not tour with The Beatles after the first US tour. In New York she had become separated from John and the boys as they were ushered into a car; later in Miami, she had trouble convincing an over-zealous security guard that she was in fact John's wife.

"We couldn't say it, but we really didn't like going back to Liverpool. Being local heroes made us nervous, and when we did shows there, they were always full of people we knew. We felt embarrassed in our suits and being very clean, because we were worried that friends might think we'd sold out – which we had in a way." — **John**

A Hard Day's Night

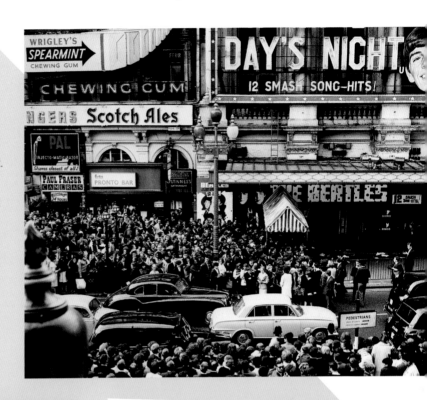

Opposite and right: Four days after their return from Australia, The Beatles attend the royal worldwide premiere of their first film *A Hard Day's Night* at the London Pavilion. John adjusts his tie as he is introduced to Princess Margaret. When asked by the Earl of Snowden what a "grotty" shirt was (a reference to a line in the film) he said, "It means simply, grotesque..." Thousands of fans gathered outside the venue to see their idols and the royal party arrive. Afterwards, while the Princess's car was stopped by fans, thinking it was The Beatles, the boys were whisked away to a celebration party in Park Lane.

Below and bottom: The Beatles play on the live ABC TV's *Blackpool Night Out*, hosted by Mike and Bernie Winters. The boys appeared alongside acts as diverse as Jimmy Edwards and Lionel Blair. Among the numbers they performed was "If I Fell", which had to be restarted when John and Paul began giggling during the opening chords.

Autumn tour 1964

Far Left: Waving goodbye to American fans as they board the plane, The Beatles return from their first full North American tour. An undoubted success, with 32 concerts in 24 cities, they played in venues across the continent from Boston on the east coast to Vancouver in Canada on the west. The *Daily Mail* called it "a bold object...to bring Beatlemania to every corner of the United States."

Left: They were in demand wherever they went from photographers, broadcasters and journalists; often they gave large press conferences to save time. Once back in Britain, the band threw themselves into a series of dates on the cinema circuit, television appearances and recording sessions in the studio. Their fourth album, *Beatles for Sale,* was released in December; a mixture of original songs and covers, John's contributions had begun to take on a more autobiographical and introspective feel, showing the influence of Bob Dylan whom he had met in New York on the recent US tour. Dylan had urged him to "listen to the words" and this was a turning point in John becoming a writer of great songs.

Below: John in costume for *Another Beatles Christmas Show* which ran from Christmas Eve 1964 through to 16 January 1965. The show was pretty much the same as the previous year with music, sketches, comedy and special guests, which included Freddie and the Dreamers and The Yardbirds. The pantomime sketch featured the boys dressed in full polar gear as Antarctic explorers searching for the abominable snowman. The rehearsals provided a chance for yet more festive fun (left inset).

Below left: As part of their British tour in the autumn, The Beatles returned to Scotland in October, this time adding two concerts at Caird Hall in Dundee to the performances in Edinburgh and Glasgow.

Opposite: John, on Wimbledon Common, filming for the first episode of *Not Only...But Also,* a comedy series starring Peter Cook and Dudley Moore. Filmed in late November and broadcast in the New Year, the scenes on the Common were to accompany a reading from John's book *In His Own Write.*

CHAPTER THREE

1965

Help me get my feet back on the ground

John had always been very fond of satire, as well as humour that played on words, and had grown up in Liverpool listening to radio programmes such as *The Goon Show*. Early in 1965 he was delighted when he appeared on Peter Cook and Dudley Moore's television programme, *Not Only… But Also*. The programme was broadcast on 9 January, and during the show John read some of his poetry. He was also a great fan of Peter Sellers' work and of Stanley Unwin a comedian who turned the English language into total double-talk – and the influence of both these performers can sometimes be seen in John's own work.

In February John passed his driving test at the first attempt – which became front-page news in the British national press. He had bought a Ferrari and a black Mini Cooper, and owned several other cars, but he was never a good driver and many of his friends had cause to regret accepting the offer of a lift home. He also had a terrible sense of direction, so almost always got lost.

At the end of that month, The Beatles began work on their second film, *Help!*, a comic strip adventure about the attempts of an obscure Middle-Eastern sect to recover a sacred sacrificial ring that a fan had sent to Ringo. This offered opportunities for location filming, so scenes in the Bahamas and Austria were written into the storyline. While in the Bahamas the group were filming in what they thought was a deserted army barracks, but John was horrified to discover that it was actually in use as a psychiatric hospital. That evening, at a black-tie dinner with the Governor, he turned on the authorities and condemned them for allowing people to live in such conditions. The local press were outraged, but John was unrepentant and delighted when the band left the Bahamas. All four Beatles had quickly become bored during the long hours of filming and had turned to smoking marijuana to fill the time, so their concentration was not 100 per cent during the making of *Help!*. Despite this, the film was completed in under three months, did very good business and was well received by the critics – although John himself never liked it much.

A Spaniard in the Works, John's second book, was published in June 1965. It was full of satire, send-ups of well-known newspaper columnists and irreverent features. In interviews at the time, he said his writing was spontaneous and undisciplined, and that he hated anything to be cut, but often added things. Although he was an avid reader he had not read many of the accepted literary greats, and denied that they had had any major influence on his work. Many of John's songs were inspired by newspaper articles – his Uncle George used to go through the paper with him when he was a young child, and had started to teach him to read using news headlines. This had instilled a lifelong interest in the news – and the habit of reading the paper – in his nephew.

Left: John performs at the Alpha TV studios in Aston, Birmingham, for the last ever Beatles' appearance on *Thank Your Lucky Stars*, in March 1965, having first appeared on the show in 1963.

John had not forgotten seeing Mimi constantly pestered by fans at Mendips the previous year. First he persuaded her to stay with him in Weybridge, then announced one morning that he was going to buy her a new house. When she was asked where she wanted to live, Mimi selected the first seaside town she could think of – and the two of them set off that morning to Bournemouth. After looking around several properties, Mimi decided she liked a bungalow overlooking Poole Harbour and within a few hours John had bought it. In a fit of sentimentality, he wanted Mimi to keep Mendips, his childhood home, but she insisted it be sold – she wanted a clean break. After she moved, John often came down to see her, relaxing and drinking tea as he watched the boats sail past. Unfortunately, Mimi did not totally escape the fans – the harbour cruises regularly came past her windows, and her house was always pointed out to the passengers.

Apart from filming and recording, John's life was still dominated by touring with The Beatles, with a European tour to France, Italy and Spain, another across America and finally a short tour around Britain. All four Beatles were beginning to feel that this endless time spent on the road, along with the suffocating adulation from the fans, was becoming almost impossible to bear. During concerts John now quite regularly told the fans to "Shaddup!" – or even worse – and even the others often stopped singing or playing for periods, since no one could have heard them anyway. The music had suffered because of the impossibility of playing well under such conditions; they had once been proud of the fact that they were a tight group of accomplished musicians, but now hardly bothered to rehearse before a tour and often ended up playing abysmally at concerts. Who could blame them, when no one seemed to be interested in listening?

During their American tour in August, John, Paul, George and Ringo finally met Elvis Presley. John in particular was a great fan of the American singer, and had copied the Elvis look and sound in the early days. The meeting was held at Elvis's Bel Air home, but it was not a great success. After some small talk they tried jamming together, then the four Beatles drifted away into the games room. A journalist instrumental in organizing the get-together said later that Elvis had been high on dope, and that the politics of the meeting had made everything too heavy.

1965 was also the year in which The Beatles received their MBEs. The announcement was met with disbelief – not only by the press, but also by the boys themselves. Some of the battle-scarred previous recipients returned their awards in disgust, but John soon pointed out that they had received theirs for killing people, while The Beatles had been

honoured for entertaining – so he thought the four of them deserved the award more. In reality, they had been honoured more for their services to the British export industry than for playing music but even so. no pop artist had received such an award before. Despite this, John initially wanted to turn the honour down as he felt it was all too Establishment; in the end he was persuaded to accept it along with the others. After the presentation he gave his medal to Mimi, who for many years kept it on top of her television in Dorset.

One predictable result of John's fame was that his missing father had reappeared on the scene. Fred Lennon turned up on the doorstep in Weybridge one day in 1965, and Cynthia had no option but to invite him in to wait for John's return. John's deeply held wish to hear about his childhood was at war with his distaste for an absentee father who had obviously come for a hand-out, and the meeting was uncomfortable and embarrassing. Fred was washing-up at a hotel in nearby Hampton Court, but he soon began talking to the press and by the end of the year had found himself a recording contract and released his own record – which did not do at all well.

Since they were disenchanted with touring, The Beatles had begun to turn their attention to pleasing themselves, rather than the public. It was no longer possible to develop new songs on the road as they had in the old days, so they looked more to the recording studio, where they were working on a more complex sound. Producer George Martin had proved to be an intuitive interpreter of their work, and his classical-music training meant he was full of ideas that were new to them. Although Lennon-McCartney still appeared on all John and Paul's compositions, as agreed in the early days, it was usually apparent who had done most of the work. Paul's lyrics went for the heart, John's made you stop and think; generally whoever sang the leading vocal had written the song.

All four Beatles now had fairly settled personal lives. Cynthia and John were an established married couple, and Julian was two years old. Ringo had married Maureen at the beginning of the year and soon they also had a son while Paul was living with Jane Asher and George with Pattie Boyd. Although this did not seem to have affected their popularity, during the height of Beatlemania the wives and girlfriends were quite often subjected to abuse and even attack from hysterical and jealous fans.

However, Beatlemania was finally beginning to show signs of running out of steam. In 1965, for the first time, some of the concert venues were not full to capacity and far fewer fans turned up at the airports to welcome the group or wave them a fond farewell. There were still plenty of fans, but perhaps they had come to realize it was a waste of money to pay for seats at a concert where their heroes could be as much as 500 yards away and at which they could not hear a note of the music. The music itself was still amazingly popular – the records sold as quickly as EMI could press them, and it was said that at any given moment in 1965, somewhere in the world a Beatles' song would be playing on the radio.

Below: Crowds gather at London Airport as The Beatles head off to the Bahamas to begin filming for their next movie, *Help!*.

Norwegian Wood

Top right & left and bottom left: Ten days after the final Christmas show, John and Cynthia, accompanied by George Martin and his wife, headed for the ski slopes of St Moritz in Switzerland. Despite appearances, John proved to be a natural skier. George Martin, however, had less luck and broke his foot on the second day of the two-week holiday. While he was recovering, John played him a song he was working on with the initial title of "This Bird Has Flown"; the song became "Norwegian Wood" and appeared on the *Rubber Soul* album.

Above: *Help!* was to be the boys' second foray into the world of feature films and was again directed by Richard Lester. It was a fantastical musical comedy adventure, which allowed them to film in exotic locations – Eleanor Bron starred alongside The Beatles and accompanied them to the Bahamas where they were to begin filming.

Above: John and Cynthia return from Switzerland where they had two weeks together uninterrupted by John's touring commitments. Four days later, on 11 February, they attended Ringo's wedding; he had proposed to Maureen Cox three weeks earlier.

John passes his test

Opposite and above: In the middle of February, John passed his driving test, the last of The Beatles to do so. Whereas the others were keen drivers, John was notoriously bad, and in fact crashed his car shortly after the test. He preferred to be driven to recording sessions and appearances.

Right: As well as filming for *Help!* and writing for the accompanying album, 1965 proved another busy year for The Beatles: European and UK tours and a return to the US were punctuated with a string of appearances on TV and radio. In between, John had been writing for their next album, *Rubber Soul*, which was released at the end of the year and contained only original material.

Below inset: On the set of *Help!* at Twickenham Studios, London, John and the boys are presented with a Radio Caroline first anniversary award by the pirate station's DJ, Simon Dee. A few days later, they topped the bill at the NME Annual Poll Winners All Star Concert at Wembley.

> Beatlemania was by no means dead, but it was ebbing… The band were actually relieved. They could move on.

John speaks his mind

Left and below: Filming for *Help!* began as soon as John and the rest of the band arrived in the Bahamas. In one scene, the boys had to emerge fully clothed from the pool at the Nassau Beach Hotel. Smoking cannabis first thing in the morning had become a norm for John and the others, and Dick Lester, the director, quickly discovered that shooting after midday was almost impossible as they would forget their lines or descend into fits of giggles.

Opposite: Keeping out of the sun. After leaving London on a cold February day, the tropical weather must have been a bonus for the boys. However, they had to seek shade for most of the time for continuity reasons. By the end of the shoot in the Bahamas, John was happy to leave, having challenged the island's Minister of Finance, at an opulent dinner, about the terrible conditions in a psychiatric hospital used for some of the filming.

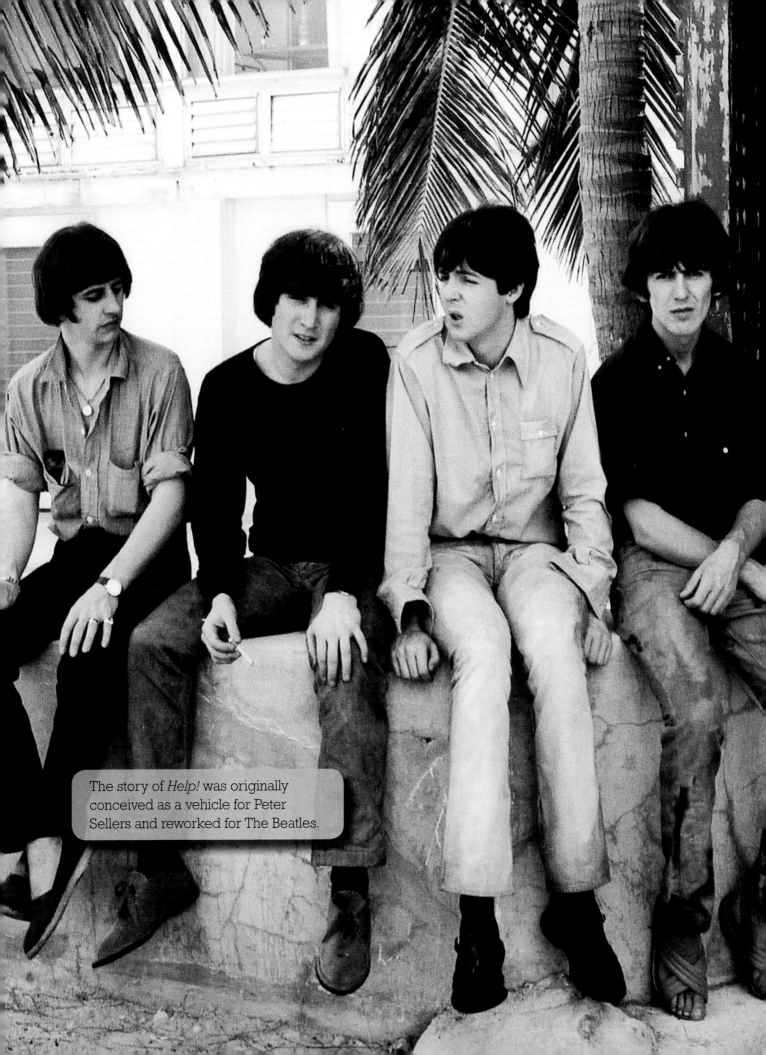

The story of *Help!* was originally conceived as a vehicle for Peter Sellers and reworked for The Beatles.

JOHN LENNON TIMELINE

1965

9 Jan John appears on Peter Cook and Dudley Moore's *Not Only...* *But Also* programme, reading his poetry.

15 Feb John passes his driving test aged 24.

9 Apr UK single release of "Ticket To Ride"/ "Yes It Is".

11 Jun It is announced at midnight that The Beatles are to receive MBEs. Two days later several recipients return their MBEs in protest.

24 Jun John's second book, *A Spaniard In The Works* is published.

23 Jul UK single release of "Help"/ "I'm Down".

29 Jul The Beatles second film, *Help!*, premieres in London.

3 Aug John buys his Aunt Mimi a bungalow in Dorset.

6 Aug Release of the album *Help!* in the UK, the first LP to go straight to number 1 in the UK charts. The album, with slightly different tracks, was issued in the US on 13 August.

15 Aug The Beatles' second US tour opens at New York's Shea Stadium to a record audience of 55,600.

26 Oct The Beatles receive their MBEs at Buckingham Palace.

3 Dec UK single release of "We Can Work It Out"/ "Day Tripper".

3 Dec UK release of the album *Rubber Soul* (6 December in the US).

31 Dec John's father, Alfred, releases his first and only single, "That's My Life (My Love And My Home)" to a poor response.

The *Help!* soundtrack was an important transitional record between the Fab era and the band's mature works.

John and Eleanor film *Help!*

Opposite and above: After a brief stopover in London, filming moved to Obertauern in Austria, before returning to London towards the end of March. The UK scenes were shot at various locations in and around Twickenham. In particular, Ailsa Avenue was used for some of the street scenes, where John was joined once more by Eleanor Bron, with whom he struck up a close friendship.

The title of The Beatles' second feature film was not settled on until seven weeks into the shoot. Both John and Paul separately wrote songs for the title track, but as with "A Hard Day's Night", John's contribution won out. Years later, he would say it was one of only two songs (the other being "Strawberry Fields Forever") he wrote "...from experience and not projecting myself into a situation and writing a nice story about it..."

Mixing John's title track

Opposite: Paul is held aloft by John and George on his 23rd birthday. The Beatles had spent the day doing final mixes for the *Help!* album to accompany the film's release. The previous day John had recorded an interview for the BBC Home Service programme *The World of Books*. The interview focused on his second book, *A Spaniard In The Works*, which was published the following week. Similar in content to *In His Own Write*, it sold reasonably well, going through four impressions. John described it as a "more complicated" book and, referring to the stories, said that "it did me good to get rid of them".

Below: In a scene from *Help!* John swaps his guitar for a horn as the boys join a marching band to disguise themselves.

Right: In another scene, on the run from murderers, John enlists the help and protection of a handful of friendly policemen.

Inset: John filming on the slopes of the ski resort of Obertauern in the Austrian Alps. The glamorous locations couldn't disguise the fact that the boys were amateurs in a film full of top-notch thespians.

The title track for the new film, *Help!*, was a genuine cry on Lennon's part.

"The plain unvarnished fact is that I like writing, and I'd go on writing even if there wasn't any publisher daft enough to publish them."
— John

"...satirical, full of whimsy but also marked by that distinctive Lennon edge"
Review of *A Spaniard in the Works*, LA Times, 8.10.2010

A Spaniard in the Works

After the publication of *In His Own Write* in March 1964, John was given just over a year to come up with a follow-up book. This would be no easy feat: *In His Own Write* was the culmination of a lifetime of musings, but the new book would have to be written with great haste.

John's second book, *A Spaniard in the Works*, was published on 24 June 1965, the title being a play on the phrase "a spanner in the works". The book was similar in character to his first book, and John admitted during an interview on the BBC Radio's *World of Books* that it was an equally undisciplined process. Some of the book had been written with the support of George during their trip to Tahiti in May 1964.

Day Tripper

Right: John and Cynthia hand-in-hand as the leave London for the Cannes Film Festival. During the year, John had been smoking a lot of marijuana but moved on to LSD when introduced to the hallucinogenic drug by dentist John Riley when he invited John, Cynthia, George and Pattie to dinner. LSD had a profound effect on John and Paul's song writing; they co-wrote "Day Tripper", which John later admitted was a drug song, although its reference was obscure enough not to tarnish their clean-cut image at the time.

Below: Paul plays and John joins in with vocals. 1965 was a busy one in the studio with two albums – *Help!* and *Rubber Soul* – released during the year. John's key contributions to *Help!*, besides the title track, were "Ticket To Ride" and "You've got to Hide Your Love Away", the latter an introspective composition inspired by Bob Dylan's work. *Rubber Soul* saw John reach a new peak in song writing. "Girl", "In My Life", "Norwegian Wood" and "Nowhere Man".

Opposite: John strikes a matador pose as he and the rest of the band return from Barcelona at the end of their European tour, which had taken them to France, Italy and Spain.

On the town

Opposite main image: John and Cynthia arrive at the royal premiere of *Help!* held at the London Pavilion on 29 July. Although fans flocked to see the film, it was less favourably received than *A Hard Day's Night*. The single "Help!" had been released the previous week and reached No. 1 in both the UK and US charts. The album, issued in August, spent 9 weeks at the top of both the UK and US charts although Capitol's version of the album was significantly different from the record released by Parlophone.

Opposite right inset below: John and the boys are presented to Princess Margaret at the premiere. She and her husband, Lord Snowden, had delayed their summer holiday for the occasion.

Opposite left inset below: Cynthia accompanies John to the premiere of Richard Lester's film *The Knack...and How to Get It*.

Left: John and Cynthia on the way to Cannes. While there, John gave an interview for CBS's *The Merv Griffin Show*, which was aired in the US a week later.

Below: The Beatles wave goodbye to their fans as they leave London Airport to begin their second tour of the US.

"*Help!* is a shiny, forgettable toy; an ideal play-with".
— Review of *Help!* by Kenneth Tynan

Above and left: John and George arrive in New York on the afternoon of 13 August. The Beatles took over an entire floor of the Warwick Hotel in Manhattan. While in the city, they appeared for the fourth and final time on *The Ed Sullivan Show* and played at the Shea Stadium.

The tour was half the length of the gruelling and sometimes chaotic 1964 marathon nevertheless, they appeared at some of the largest venues they had ever played. Vast crowds turned out but the stadiums were rarely full. Despite this, the noise generated by the fans meant The Beatles could have played anything – or even stopped playing! – and nobody would have noticed. Their feelings of disillusionment and frustration over touring intensified during the US tour.

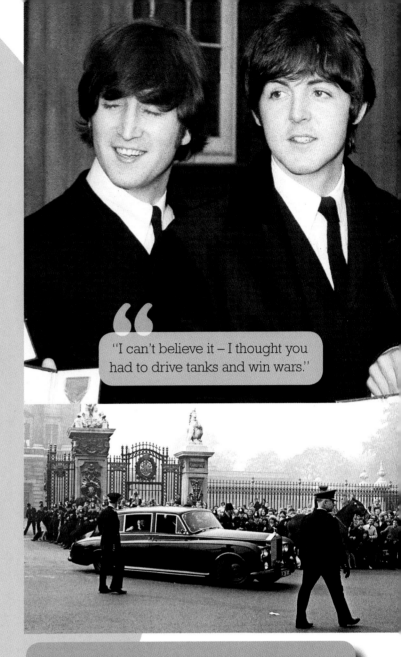

John's honour

This page: In June 1965 The Beatles had been awarded MBEs in the Queen's Birthday Honours List on the recommendation of Harold Wilson, the Prime Minister. Initially, they had considered declining the awards but were persuaded otherwise on the basis of their contribution to Britain's economy through their overseas earnings. There was a backlash from the press and the public, with some war veterans returning theirs in protest at a mere pop group being honoured in such a way. John, as acerbic as ever, pointed out that many of the veterans would have won their awards for killing people; whereas the Beatles had been given theirs for entertaining people. "On balance, I'd say we deserve ours more", he concluded. On 26 October they attended the investiture at Buckingham Palace, where a crowd turned out to greet them. Brian Epstein accompanied them to the Palace. Four years later, John returned his MBE in protest against, among other things, Britain's support of the Nigerian government in the Biafran War.

Four years later, John returned his MBE in protest against, among other things, Britain's support of the Nigerian government in the Biafran War.

Lennon and McCartney

Above: A striking portrait of Lennon by photographer and friend Robert Whitaker. The Beatles were unusual in the pop world in the early 1960s because they wrote their own songs. John had previously written for other artists and showed a desire to be more involved in the production side. The less frenetic pace of 1965, compared to 1964, had allowed him to focus more on his song writing and studio work for both the *Help!* and *Rubber Soul* albums. The latter had seen The Beatles employ new studio techniques, such as multi-tracking and tape loops. As the year came to an end, the boys had completed their last ever UK tour; the following year would see them spend more time in the studio and announce the end of their touring days.

Opposite: A group of showgirls surround John and Paul during rehearsals for *The Music of Lennon and McCartney*, a special programme broadcast by Granada TV. Appearing on the bill alongside The Beatles were Cilla Black, Peter and Gordon, Lulu and Marianne Faithfull. Filmed in November, it was broadcast on 16 December.

CHAPTER FOUR

1966

Try to see it my way

By now John wanted to stop touring, as did George. Their music was suffering because of the conditions they had to work under; the relentless attention of the fans was becoming more like terrorization than adoration – but another factor in their reluctance to continue was that they both hated flying. Both Paul and Ringo wanted to carry on; Paul was a showman who liked to play in front of an audience and Ringo just enjoyed being on the road. While they argued it out between themselves, the first few months of 1966 were spent in the recording studio, working on a whole host of new material.

In June they set off on a short tour of Germany, Japan and the Philippines, which was a disaster from start to finish. In Hamburg, where they were welcomed back with open arms, John told the audience not to listen to The Beatles' music any more, because it was terrible now. The fans were deeply upset – although what he had really meant was that he thought they had lost the edge and excitement of the early Hamburg days.

In Japan, they had been booked into the Nippon Budokan, which was dedicated to traditional martial arts and had never been used for anything else. Many Japanese considered it a sacred building and were horrified it was to be the venue for a pop concert; opposition was bitter and there were angry demonstrations and marches. Because of fears for their safety, The Beatles were confined to their hotel under armed guard. Of course John managed to slip away, but was promptly rounded up and returned, along with threats that all security would be withdrawn if they didn't all toe the line. At the concert itself, the fans were kept strictly in order, so they sat quietly and listened to the music. Unfortunately, since the band were expecting the usual mayhem in which no one could hear them, they had again not bothered to rehearse and it was immediately apparent that almost everything was mis-timed or off-key. The fans probably did not care, but it brought home to John and the others just how far their levels of musicianship had slipped.

In Manila they inadvertently missed a reception given by Imelda Marcos, which was taken by the locals as a snub to the President's wife. Ferdinand and Imelda Marcos were at the height of their power, and an apparent insult was not going to be taken lightly. Although there were no problems at the concerts, The Beatles were jeered as they left for the airport, security was withdrawn and they were jostled by men with guns. On their return to England, John told the waiting press, "When they started on us at the airport, I was petrified. I thought I was going to get hurt, so I headed for three nuns and two monks, thinking that if I was close to these people that might stop them."

All this was as nothing compared with the storm that broke over their heads in America in August, due to remarks that John had made four months earlier in England. He had been interviewed for the *Evening Standard* newspaper, during the course of which he commented that Christianity was vanishing and that The Beatles were now more popular than Jesus. He apparently meant that Christianity was in such a state that groups such as The Beatles were better known than Jesus. His remarks were part of a much longer piece and passed without comment in Britain, but at the end of July the article was

Opposite: A pensive John pictured after the press conference in Chicago, held to allow him to explain his remarks about Jesus.

reprinted in the American magazine *Datebook*, under a syndication arrangement. This time they were taken out of context, and front-page headlines screamed that John had claimed that The Beatles were bigger than Jesus Christ. The American Bible Belt reacted with fury, with Beatles merchandise being ceremoniously burned and their music banned on an estimated thirty-five radio stations across several states. It all happened just days before the group was due to start an American tour. John was not concerned at first, and refused to back down, but it soon became evident that the anti-Beatles campaign was deadly serious and would be long-term unless something was done. At a quickly arranged press conference in Chicago at the start of the tour, John attempted to explain his remarks – but journalists refused to be placated until he apologized. Under pressure he did so, although privately he was still convinced that he had not said anything that he needed to apologize for. He did have one unexpected ally, in the shape of the Bishop of Montreal, the Rt Rev. Kenneth Maguire, who said, "I wouldn't be surprised if The Beatles actually were more popular than Jesus. In the only popularity poll in Jesus's time, he came out second best to Barabbas."

The tour went ahead, but it was to be their last. The magic had gone and now perhaps it was actively dangerous. During the recent pandemonium they had all received death threats, and it was still possible that someone out there would refuse to accept the apology – when a firecracker exploded on stage in Memphis, each of them looked to see which one had been shot. When he returned to Britain, John told Cynthia he was pleased that the touring was over, but privately he did not know how to move forward. The Beatles had always been a touring band – now what would they do? He had achieved everything he had set out to do, and more, in just six years – and now he didn't know what he wanted next.

While he considered what to do about his future, he took his first solo film role – the part of Private Gripweed in *How I Won the War*. At the beginning of September he flew to Celle, West Germany, to begin filming – but first he had to look the part. His Beatle locks were all shorn off in a regulation army haircut – and he acquired the famous wire-framed "granny glasses". Ironically, John had refused to wear similar spectacles when he was first diagnosed as short-sighted, but now they became his trademark – and they instantly became fashionable among style-conscious young people everywhere. John enjoyed the experience of working on *How I Won the War* but found the endless waiting around on set boring, while his attention span was too short to learn anything but the shortest lines. He could have been a fine actor – but he decided that it was not the life for him.

John had been introduced to LSD in 1965. It detached him from the mundane world, heightened his perceptions, and freed him from responsibility. One benefit to those around him was that he was less quick to lash out with his sharp tongue, and he became softer and less confrontational. He tried to persuade Cynthia to take LSD too, but after one bad trip she refused to touch it again. From then on they were travelling in different directions; it was the beginning of the end of their marriage.

Meanwhile, John had become more involved with the art world. It had been his first love before music, and now he began to take an interest again and started to attend exhibitions and art-world parties. Cynthia was happy to stay at home, so John often went to these events alone. At the beginning of November he was invited to a private preview of *Unfinished Paintings and Objects* by conceptual artist Yoko Ono. As he studied the exhibits, Yoko walked up to him and gave him a card, on which was printed the word "Breathe". One exhibit involved climbing a stepladder and hammering a nail into the wall. John asked if he could try it, but Yoko was reluctant, because the exhibition had not yet opened. Finally she said he could, if he paid five shillings. Quick as a flash, John replied, "I'll give you an imaginary five shillings, and I'll hammer in an imaginary nail." He thought the whole thing was "nutty" – but it was fascinating as well. The two of them enjoyed the same mind-games and they could each feel the spark of attraction – even though they were both still married to other people.

In November John appeared again in Peter Cook and Dudley Moore's programme, *Not Only … But Also*. This time he was in one of the sketches, playing the commissionaire of a "members only" club. The programme was broadcast on BBC television on 26 December, and it represented John's last solo acting performance.

During 1966 The Beatles released several singles, two EPs and two LPs, and at the end of the year they were recording another single, "Strawberry Fields Forever". However, that Christmas, for the first time in three years, there was no new Beatles' album ready for release. In Britain, EMI compromised by collecting together some of the best songs and releasing *A Collection of Beatles Oldies*. Although they were no longer touring, The Beatles had by no means split up – but effectively they now only existed as a group in the recording studio.

Above: The Beatles at rehearsals for their only live appearance on *Top of the Pops* on 16 June. They mimed to both sides of their new single – "Paperback Writer" and "Rain". The double-tracking on "Paperback Writer" made it tricky to perform live; similarly, "Rain", written by John, featured backward guitar and vocals in the fade-out, an effect difficult to reproduce in the television studio. Lennon claimed to have discovered the effect by accident, when, high on marijuana, he had threaded a rough mix tape the wrong way round. The distorted and dreamy lyrics gave a feeling of being detached from the real world, similar to that experienced through LSD, which John had been introduced to the previous year.

"He is very keen on books, will always ask what is good to read. He buys quantities of books and these are kept tidily in a special room. He has Swift, Tennyson, Huxley, Orwell, costly leather-bound editions of Tolstoy, Oscar Wilde. Then there's *Little Women* and all the William books from his childhood."
Maureen Cleave interview, *Evening Standard*, 4 March 1966

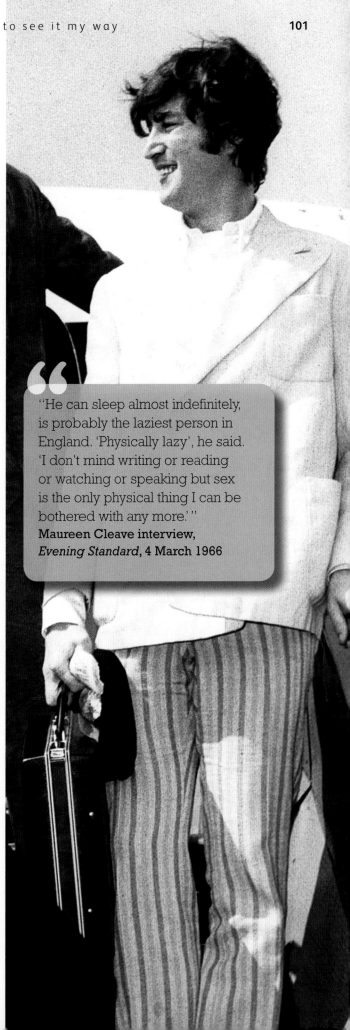

"He can sleep almost indefinitely, is probably the laziest person in England. 'Physically lazy', he said. 'I don't mind writing or reading or watching or speaking but sex is the only physical thing I can be bothered with any more.'"
Maureen Cleave interview,
Evening Standard, **4 March 1966**

Final world tour

This spread: In the spring of 1966, John and the rest of the band spent an intensive ten weeks in the studio recording tracks for their next album, *Revolver*, their most ambitious to date and one in which Lennon was able to begin experimenting with sound in the studio. Before *Revolver* was released, the band embarked on what turned out to be their final world tour, beginning in June with Germany and their old haunt of Hamburg. This was their first return to the city since 1962 and they arrived in style to an enthusiastic welcome from the German fans. Despite this, none of the band relished the idea of performing live; the recording of *Revolver* had fired their enthusiasm for studio work. None of the new material was included in the 11-song set for the tour.

The two shows in Hamburg were their first return to the city since Christmas 1962.

John in Japan

Below: After Hamburg, the boys continued their world tour in Japan, where Beatlemania was thriving. But the trip was not without controversy – unbeknown to John and the rest of the band, the Nippon Budokan Hall, where all five of their concerts were played, was a sacred martial arts venue. A substantial protest against what was seen as an act of cultural vandalism, led for the most part by a militant student faction, meant that for the 10,000 fans, the Japanese authorities had to lay on 3,000 police officers to protect The Beatles. The concerts themselves were a strange experience for the band, who were used to screaming hysteria from their fans; instead they were met by a polite, subdued audience kept under control by the massive police presence.

Left: Prior to the start of the tour, The Beatles perform live at the NME Poll Winners Concert at Wembley in May. Although it wasn't known at the time, the 15-minute set at the Empire Pool was to be the band's last concert performance on British soil. The event was filmed by ABC TV but the cameras had been turned off when the Beatles performed.

> It should have been the highlight of the televised show but The Beatles' last home performance was not recorded for posterity.

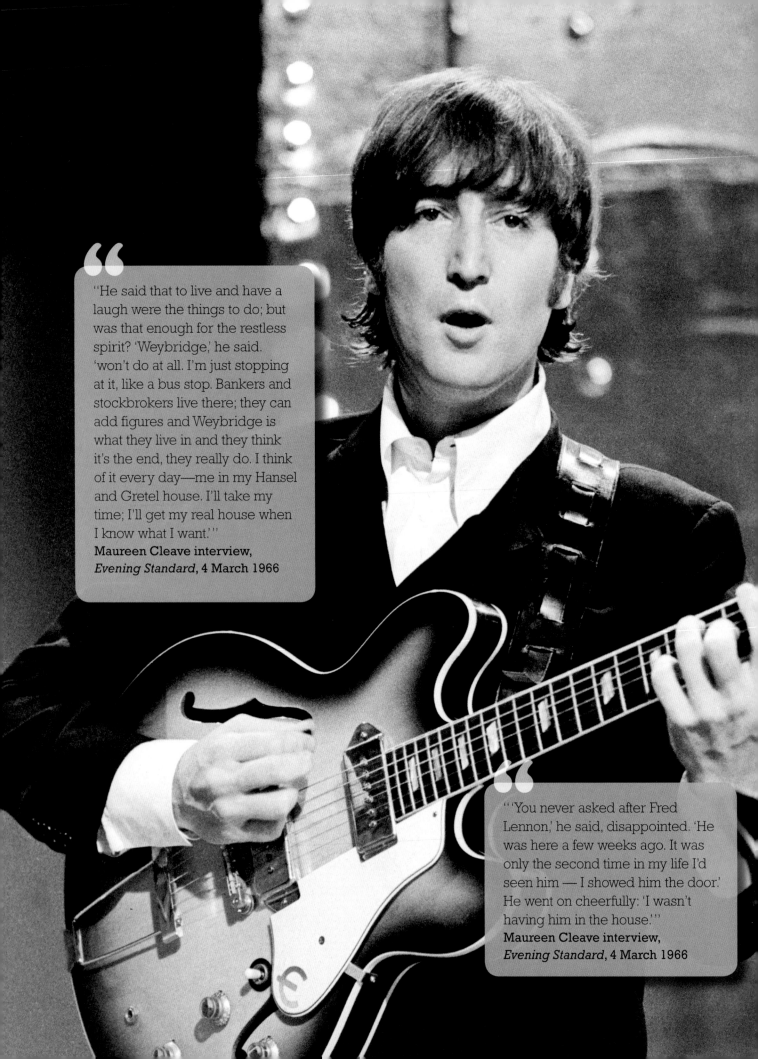

"He said that to live and have a laugh were the things to do; but was that enough for the restless spirit? 'Weybridge,' he said. 'won't do at all. I'm just stopping at it, like a bus stop. Bankers and stockbrokers live there; they can add figures and Weybridge is what they live in and they think it's the end, they really do. I think of it every day—me in my Hansel and Gretel house. I'll take my time; I'll get my real house when I know what I want.'"

Maureen Cleave interview, *Evening Standard*, 4 March 1966

"'You never asked after Fred Lennon,' he said, disappointed. 'He was here a few weeks ago. It was only the second time in my life I'd seen him — I showed him the door.' He went on cheerfully: 'I wasn't having him in the house.'"

Maureen Cleave interview, *Evening Standard*, 4 March 1966

John in the Philippines

Next stop was the Philippines, where controversy was ratcheted up and the boys came under more hostile fire from the press and the public. As The Beatles landed, the *Manila Sunday Times* ran a story declaring the band were to meet with the First Lady, Imelda Marcos; the tight schedule in Manila meant such a visit had already been ruled out by Brian Epstein, little realizing the offence and public backlash it would cause. Newspaper headlines declared Imelda had been "stood up"; the snub led to ugly scenes at the airport as the band departed, where the usual official protection was withdrawn and John and the rest of the band were subjected to verbal and physical abuse. When told by an official that they were being treated like ordinary passengers, John commented that he hoped getting punched, kicked and spat at wasn't the usual experience for ordinary passengers!

Top left: On their return to Britain, the band hold a press conference about their experience; John told the waiting journalists, "When they started on us at the airport, I was petrified. I thought I was going to get hurt, so I headed for three nuns and two monks, thinking that if I was close to these people that might stop them."

Middle left: The world tour continued as the boys flew to the US. Delayed in London, they are given a tour of the airport.

Below: Fans gather at London Airport to bid farewell to The Beatles as they embark on the last leg of their world tour. There is some apprehension about their reception in the States following the republication of John's remarks about "Jesus" two weeks earlier.

"I was very delicate and moved every time they touched me. I was petrified."

"We'll just never go to any nuthouses again."

"'You get treated like ordinary passenger', they were saying; ordinary passenger? He doesn't get kicked does he?"

It was taken wrong...

In early March 1966, John had given an interview to Maureen Cleave of the *Evening Standard*. Headlined "How Does a Beatle Live?" it covered a range of lifestyle topics; within it was a quote from John where he talked about the disappearance of Christianity and the transience of rock and roll, uttering the now famous words: "We're more popular than Jesus right now. I don't know which will go first, rock'n'roll or Christianity."

The remarks passed largely without comment at the time but two weeks before the start of the US tour, they were republished in *Datebook*, a US teen magazine. The reaction this time around was immense; Christian fundamentalists in the US stirred the issue into a ferment. Beatles' records were banned across radio stations, primarily in the south, and public burnings of their records took place.

Right: John pictured prior to setting off for the US in August.

Inset: John surrounded by the press and state troopers as he arrives in Chicago for the start of the US tour.

Bottom: John looking pensive prior to the press conference in Chicago. Initially refusing to apologize for his remarks, he was persuaded to show some repentance, although his carefully worded remarks stopped short of a full-blown apology.

"Christianity will go. It will vanish and shrink. I needn't argue with that; I'm right and I will be proved right. We're more popular than Jesus now; I don't know which will go first — rock and roll or Christianity. Jesus was all right, but his disciples were thick and ordinary. It's them twisting it that ruins it for me."
Maureen Cleave interview, *Evening Standard,* **4 March 1966**

"I suppose if I had said television was more popular than Jesus, I would have gotten away with it. I'm sorry I opened my mouth. I'm not anti-God, anti-Christ, or anti-religion. I wasn't knocking it or putting it down. I was just saying it as a fact and it's true more for England than here. I'm not saying that we're better or greater, or comparing us with Jesus Christ as a person or God as a thing or whatever it is. I just said what I said and it was wrong. Or it was taken wrong. And now it's all this."
—**John**

JOHN LENNON TIMELINE

1966

4 Mar The *Evening Standard* publishes an interview with John, reported by Maureen Cleave, in which he states that The Beatles are "more popular than Jesus".

10 Jun UK single release of "Paperback Writer"/ "Rain".

29 Jul The Maureen Cleave interview is published in US teen magazine *Datebook*.

31 Jul Radio stations in the US "Bible Belt"' ban The Beatles, and bonfires of their records and memorabilia are organized as a reaction to John's comments.

5 Aug "Revolver", the seventh studio album, is released accompanied by the UK single release of "Eleanor Rigby"/ "Yellow Submarine".

6 Aug Brian Epstein holds a press conference in New York to explain John's "Jesus" comments.

11 Aug The Beatles fly to Chicago for the start of what is to prove their final US tour.

12 Aug Supported by the rest of the group, John faces the American press to explain and apologize for his remarks.

29 Aug The Beatles make their last stage appearance at San Francisco's Candlestick Park.

5 Sept John goes to Celle in West Germany to begin filming his part in *How I Won the War*, where he is to acquire his trademark spectacles.

9 Nov John meets the conceptual artist Yoko Ono at her exhibition *Unfinished Paintings and Objects* at the Indica Gallery, London.

27 Nov John films a sketch for *Not Only...But Also*, to be broadcast on Christmas Day.

"I wasn't saying whatever they are saying I was saying. I was sort of deploring the attitude towards Christianity. I'm sorry. I'm sorry I said it really. I never meant it as a religious thing." —John

"I reckon we could send out four waxwork dummies of ourselves and that would satisfy the crowds. Beatles concerts are nothing to do with music anymore. They're just bloody tribal rites." —John

Finally... Candlestick Park

The US tour was successful but not a sell-out. Fears for their safety were probably uppermost on the boys' minds. Alongside the animosity and death threats, in Cleveland fans almost broke through the security cordons and the concert came to a halt as the boys left the stage; in Memphis, a firecracker exploded during the performance, unnerving John who thought he had been shot at; the Ku Klux Klan staged a protest outside the Washington DC gig; the Cincinnati concert had to be cancelled because of bad weather; by the time the band reached the last venue of the tour – Candlestick Park in San Francisco – they all agreed their touring days were at an end.

Opposite, below left and below inset: Returning home at the end of the US tour, the band were relieved to touch down on British soil. John, in particular, had become disillusioned by the slog of touring and the fact that they were playing to audiences who did not appear to want to listen to their music. He later wrote: "I always remember to thank Jesus for the end of my touring days; if I hadn't said The Beatles were "bigger than Jesus"... I might still be up there with all the other performing fleas!"

Beatle fans back as Lennon says 'I'm sorry'

From JEFFREY BLYTH
NEW YORK, Friday

AMERICAN teenagers, at least in Chicago, have forgiven the Beatles.

Twenty-six thousand fans are expected at the first two concerts of their new American tour. Both concerts are a sell-out.

Today several hundred fans, mostly girls, gathered outside the Beatles' hotel waiting for a glimpse of them leaving for their concerts. There were no anti-Beatle demonstrations.

On their arrival in Chicago late last night John Lennon gave a semi-apology for his remarks on the comparative popularity of the Beatles and Christianity.

Worried

"I wasn't saying whatever they are saying I was saying," he declared. "I was sort of deploring the attitude towards Christianity.

"I'm sorry. I'm sorry I said it really. I never meant it as a lousy, anti-religious thing."

All the Beatles admitted they had been worried by the outbreak of record burning following republication of John Lennon's comments in an American teenage magazine.

In Birmingham, Alabama: Disc jockey Tommy Charles, who started the "Ban the Beatles" campaign over Lennon's remarks, said today that he accepted Lennon's apology and would call off an anti-Beatles bonfire.

> "I was always waiting for a reason to get out of The Beatles from the day I made *How I Won the War* in 1966." —**John**

How I Won The War

Opposite and this page: Although John was almost certainly the most independent of The Beatles, and had longed for an end to touring, now that the madness of life on the road had come to an end he was faced with the problem of how to fill his time. He spent a few days immersed in domestic routine at Weybridge with Cynthia and Julian, but less than a week after returning from the North American tour, he was off again. This time he travelled to Hanover in West Germany to begin work on his first solo movie role, as Private Gripweed in Dick Lester's anti-war satire *How I Won the War*. The part required an army regulation haircut for John, and also the donning of a pair of National Health Service spectacles, which soon became something of a trademark.

While in Spain, he was visited by Cynthia as well as Ringo and Maureen but John also used the spare time during filming to write songs, beginning work on "Strawberry Fields Forever".

John meets Yoko

Top left and bottom left: John and Cynthia arrive back from Spain in early November 1966, after John had completed filming for *How I Won the War*. Although the experience had not been entirely satisfactory, and would in fact prove to be John's only film role without his fellow Beatles, the anti-war sentiment of the movie certainly appealed to him. At this time John was still yet to publicly denounce the war in Vietnam and to find fame as a peace campaigner, but he could soon be seen sporting the badge of the Campaign for Nuclear Disarmament. Toward the end of the month, guitar in hand, and armed with the bare bones of "Strawberry Fields Forever," John returned to the Abbey Road studios to be reunited with his bandmates for a recording session. The song, which combined nostalgic yearning with LSD-inspired, hallucinatory imagery, proved to be one of The Beatles' most complex recordings and, for many, one of their best.

Below right and opposite: Just two days after returning from Spain, John Lennon opted out of a party held by Brian Epstein for The Who and instead attended a preview of an avant-garde exhibition at the fashionable Indica Gallery in St James's, where the Japanese conceptual artist Yoko Ono was showing *Unfinished Paintings and Objects*. He was introduced to her by the gallery's owner, John Dunbar. Although the two did not meet again for several months, the connection was made. John later recalled the moment: "...that's when we really met. That's when we locked eyes and she got it and I got it and that was it."

Although it would be some time before they would renew their acquaintance, the connection between John and Yoko was made.

"They keep telling me I'm all right for money but then I think I may have spent it all by the time I'm 40 so I keep going. That's why I started selling my cars; then I changed my mind and got them all back and a new one too."
Maureen Cleave interview,
Evening Standard, 4 March 1966.

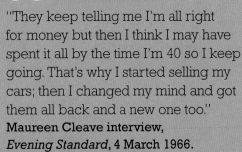

Working with Peter Cook

Above and opposite: John makes a second cameo appearance on the Peter Cook and Dudley Moore comedy show *Not Only...But Also*. He played the role of a doorman at the fictional gentlemen's club, Ad Lav, a pun on the name of the Ad Lib Club, a fashionable London venue he and the other Beatles had often visited. The sketch was filmed at the entrance to an underground men's toilets in Soho. Peter Cook also featured in the sketch as the Duke and Duchess of Windsor. This represented John's last solo acting peformance. During filming he had become particularly friendly with Peter Cook, since they shared a similar sense of humour.

CHAPTER FIVE

1967

All you need is love

After their first meeting, Yoko sent John a copy of her book, *Grapefruit*, which was quickly followed by a stream of postcards simply printed with instructions such as, "Dance", "Watch All the Lights Until Dawn", and "Hit a Wall with Your Head". Although John thought they were weird, they caught his imagination and made him think. Cynthia had always accepted that John had affairs while he was away touring – and in fact early in 1967 he told her that he had often been unfaithful – but her attitude was that since he always came back, the odd fling was not significant in their relationship. Despite the fact that she was now married to a millionaire who was famous all round the world, essentially Cynthia had changed very little over the past six years. She was a wife and mother, and saw her role as providing stable roots for her husband, looking after their son and running their home. However, John had changed – and although there was nothing really wrong with his marriage, now he wanted something more. His relationship with Yoko took months to develop – but he was quickly intrigued by the tiny woman, with her long black hair and petite figure.

On the business front, John, Paul, George and Ringo had recently formed The Beatles & Co., a legal partnership to handle all their business affairs, which bound them together until 1977. Like John, the other three Beatles were also looking for new interests now they were no longer touring. Paul wrote music for a film and tried painting, George became interested in India and its religions and music, Ringo began to spend more time with his family. However, despite the different directions they were moving in, they still wanted to be together to make music and for some time they had been working in the recording studio in earnest to produce their next LP, *Sgt. Pepper's Lonely Hearts Club Band*. It proved to be a revolutionary step forward in their musical development and was instantly acclaimed by the critics, who believed it set exciting new standards for popular music. Since it was the period of flower-power, love and peace, *Sgt. Pepper* quickly became the sound track to Swinging London. The Lennon-McCartney partnership was now no longer really a partnership at all, as each was developing his skill in a very different way; John was becoming introspective and writing psychedelic and disorientating lyrics, while Paul's songs were much more bright, breezy and commercial.

The Beatles' "loveable moptop" image took rather a battering in May 1967, when "A Day in the Life" from *Sgt. Pepper* became the first Beatles song to be banned by the BBC, because of its supposed drug references. The powers that be had taken exception to the words, "went upstairs and had a smoke". Soon afterwards, Paul admitted on television that he had taken LSD and the following month John and the others signed a petition published in *The Times*, calling for the legalization of marijuana. The press were quick to condemn them, but for many young people it just added to The Beatles' appeal.

Despite the controversy, The Beatles still held an unassailable position in popular culture, and they were chosen to compose a song for the *Our World* television show, which was to be broadcast on a global link-up across the world

Opposite: John at the launch party for *Sgt Pepper*, sporting the latest in psychedelic fashion; he and the other Beatles had embraced the popular hippie counter-culture embodied in the "Summer of Love" phenomenon of spiritualism, psychedelia and anti-war views.

in June. The brief was for something simple, suitable for varying cultures, and John came up with "All You Need is Love". Despite the importance of the occasion, the composer played it cool and chewed gum as he sang before 400 million people across five continents. The song went on to top the charts and became the anthem for the hippie generation. The broadcast was significant for another reason as well: it was the last time The Beatles appeared together live on television.

That summer, John decided it might be a great idea if The Beatles bought themselves a Greek island, where they could all go to escape the endless intrusions on their privacy. He complained that fans still seemed to think that his home was some sort of holiday park, and constantly camped outside with flasks of tea and sandwiches hoping to get a glimpse of him. He and the others went to Greece to begin negotiating, but they all pulled out of the deal when it became apparent that Greek officials were planning to use it for propaganda purposes.

John, Paul and George were still looking for some sort of meaning to life, and in August they were all introduced to the Maharishi Mahesh Yogi, during his visit to London, by George's wife, Pattie. All four Beatles threw themselves behind his movement and they soon decided to follow him to Bangor in Wales to study Transcendental Meditation. Cynthia managed to miss the train taking them all and arrived later, to be berated by John to the point of tears for always being late. It underlined the growing split in their marriage.

While they were in Wales, news came of Brian Epstein's death from an accidental overdose of sleeping tablets. Despite their rather laid-back public response to the news, they were all devastated. John, in particular, felt that without a manager to lead and organize them they were finished. At an emergency meeting held at Paul's house a few days after Brian's death, they discussed their future. Paul took charge and suggested that they should start work on a project that had been postponed for some time: the filming of the *Magical Mystery Tour*.

The basis of this project was that they should all pile into a bus with a film crew and various other passengers, and just drive round southern England filming the adventures they were sure to have. There was no firm script, no experienced director and no one had any idea what they were doing. John went along with the concept, although he resented Paul assuming leadership of The Beatles. The resulting ten hours of film took eleven weeks to edit down into the final one-hour version, and the entire project cost in the region of £75,000. When it was shown on BBC television at Christmas it was savagely criticized; John dubbed it "the most expensive home movie ever".

Soon after they returned from filming *Magical Mystery Tour* in the West Country, an exhibition of Yoko's work opened at London's Lisson Art Gallery. It was called *Half-Wind Show*, and it consisted of several everyday objects – a chair, washbasin, pillow – all cut in half. The show was subtitled *Yoko plus Me*: the "Me" was John, who had sponsored it, but insisted on remaining anonymous and did not attend. He was beginning to quietly move away from his rather conventional home life in stockbroker Surrey – the signs were already becoming apparent for anyone who cared to look. He was increasingly involved with the art world and his drug-taking was becoming extremely heavy, despite Cynthia's disapproval. The other homes around theirs were boringly staid, but their garden now sported a traditional wooden gypsy caravan, which was painted in psychedelic colours, and his sober black Rolls-Royce was given a brilliantly coloured paint job to match. John had always had an individualistic streak, but his increasing involvement with Yoko was now giving him the confidence and impetus to break out of the pattern he had been forced into by circumstances, and do his own thing.

Meanwhile, The Beatles as a group had moved on to other things. They now saw themselves as businessmen, building their own empire in which they would be in total control. The first manifestation of this was the Apple Boutique, opened on Baker Street at the beginning of December 1967. The Apple organization was not intended solely to handle their own business interests; both Paul and George hoped that it would also operate philanthropically to foster new talent. John was not as convinced as the others about this side of things, but accepted that something had to be put in place to run their affairs now that Brian Epstein was dead. He and George, along with Cynthia and Pattie, were the only two Beatles at the Apple Boutique opening party. The launch was attended by most of London society, but the general public stayed away from the shop in droves and it was not long before it failed.

John and George were still interested in meditation and in the Maharishi, and they did much to popularize his cause amongst young people. They both appeared in public with him several times, including on *The Frost Programme* on ITV and at a UNICEF gala in Paris.

To all intents and purposes, The Beatles still appeared very much together – at the premiere of John's film, *How I Won the War*, in London, all four Beatles with their wives and girlfriends attended. In reality, they were all constantly growing further apart and it was not long before the differences between them were to become very apparent.

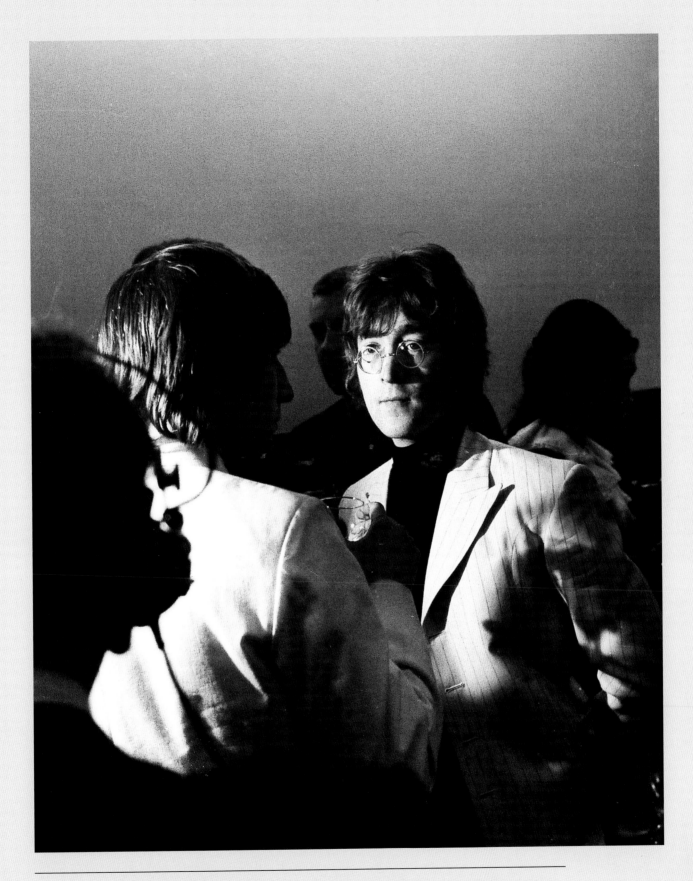

Above: John attends the opening party for the Apple Boutique on 5 December at Baker Street, London. Described as a "psychedelic Garden of Eden for lovers of hippie gear", it was one of the first business ventures by the Beatles' Apple Corps.

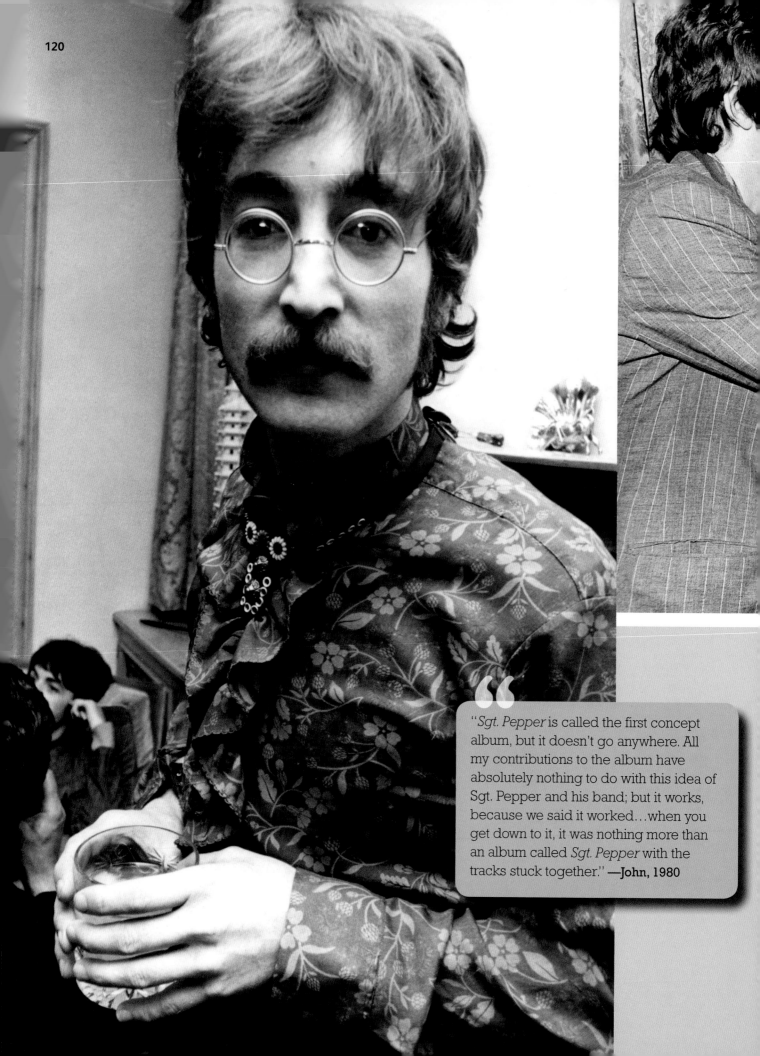

"*Sgt. Pepper* is called the first concept album, but it doesn't go anywhere. All my contributions to the album have absolutely nothing to do with this idea of Sgt. Pepper and his band; but it works, because we said it worked…when you get down to it, it was nothing more than an album called *Sgt. Pepper* with the tracks stuck together." —**John, 1980**

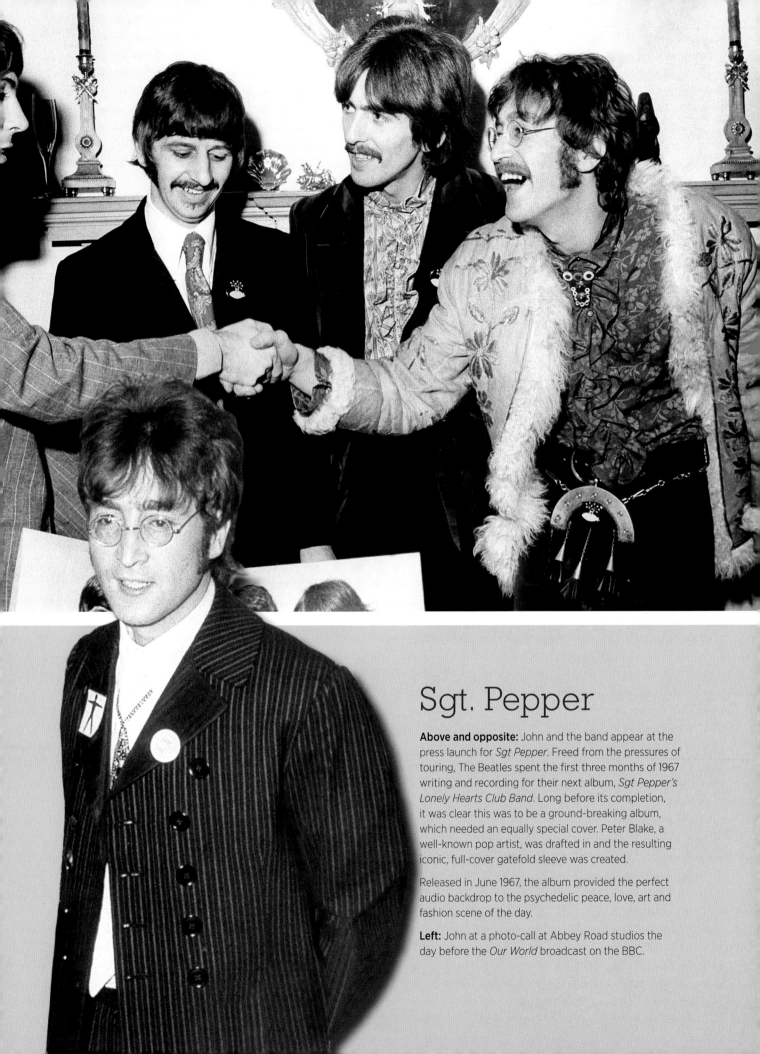

Sgt. Pepper

Above and opposite: John and the band appear at the press launch for *Sgt Pepper*. Freed from the pressures of touring, The Beatles spent the first three months of 1967 writing and recording for their next album, *Sgt Pepper's Lonely Hearts Club Band*. Long before its completion, it was clear this was to be a ground-breaking album, which needed an equally special cover. Peter Blake, a well-known pop artist, was drafted in and the resulting iconic, full-cover gatefold sleeve was created.

Released in June 1967, the album provided the perfect audio backdrop to the psychedelic peace, love, art and fashion scene of the day.

Left: John at a photo-call at Abbey Road studios the day before the *Our World* broadcast on the BBC.

A Day in John's Life

Above: At times John was content to spend time with Julian, read, watch television, or write music in his home studio. During the days of touring he often longed to be at home, but after spending so much time on the road he invariably found it difficult to adjust to domestic life upon his return, quickly becoming bored and restless. With touring over, John increasingly turned to LSD to fill the void, but while he could lose himself in psychedelic experiences, constant tripping did nothing to alleviate his insecurities.

Opposite: At a photo-call for the *Our World* broadcast. In June 1967, all four Beatles appeared on the world's first live televised satellite link-up, *Our World*. The event was viewed by around 400 million people worldwide across five continents, John wrote "All You Need is Love" especially for the occasion. The band performed live with a 13-piece orchestra, although a backing track had been pre-recorded.

Right inset: When John claims to have "read the news today" in the song "A Day in the Life", it was the *Daily Mail* of 17 January that he had in mind. This article on page seven provided the famous lyrics about counting all the small holes in the road in Blackburn, Lancashire.

FAR&NEAR

The holes in our roads

THERE are 4,000 holes in the road in Blackburn, Lancashire, or one twenty-sixth of a hole per person, according to a council survey.

If Blackburn is typical there are two million holes in Britain's roads and 300,000 in London.

£225,0000 sea defence scheme for Felixstowe is being urged on the Government by East Suffolk River Board.

1,000 ratepayers in Harrow, Middlesex, said the Exchequer should pay for education and the police.

Four Australian State Ministers began a three-week tour of Britain.

Trotting ground will be opened by Bournemouth council.

Council tenants in Ipswich will protest at a public meeting against a 25 p.c. rent rise.

Round-Britain walker Frank Haines, 23, of Rugby, is to walk across the U.S.A.

Chairman of Petworth rural council, Sussex, for 20 years, Major George Mant, 71, died.

British Red Cross has sent £1,000 to Malaysian flood victims.

Farmers will be asked to give

Our World 1967

Above left: John stands behind sandwich-boards, spelling out "All You Need is Love" in English, French, German and Spanish, at the Abbey Road studios as the band prepare for the *Our World* event.

Left: Through a mutual acquaintance at the Indica Gallery, John had met John Alexis Mardas, a Greek electronics wizard, whom he had dubbed "Magic Alex". Taken with Alex's surreal ideas and on a suggestion from him, John had hit upon the idea of The Beatles buying a Greek island to set up a commune away from the prying eyes of the press and public. John and Paul flew to Greece in July to join Ringo and George. Negotiations reached an advanced stage but the deal collapsed when it became apparent that the Greek government was using the deal for PR purposes. The boys returned to Britain empty-handed, even though British newspapers reported they had bought an Aegean island for £150,000.

Above and opposite: John, kitted out in flower-power gear, returns to Britain from Greece with Julian and Cynthia at the end of July. John's use of LSD had continued and increased, whereas Cynthia, having taken the hallucinogenic drug and experienced bad trips, had rejected it. This proved to be another distancing between them: John embraced psychedelia and its other worldliness, while Cynthia looked to provide a stable and more "normal" lifestyle for the family. For the time being, however, they continued to spend time together at home and take trips abroad.

> John's latest brainchild was for the four of them to set up an island commune.

"All You Need is Love" put The Beatles back on top of the UK chart and became the enduring anthem for the flower-power generation.

John and the Maharishi

Opposite and above: John returning from Greece – still in search of a greater meaning in his life. He was introduced to Transcendental Meditation by George and Pattie Harrison, both of whom were seeking spiritual enlightenment away from LSD and marijuana. George in particular was attracted to eastern mysticism and fully embraced the teachings of the Indian guru Maharishi Mahesh Yogi.

Right and top left: John and The Beatles attend a lecture given by the Maharishi at the London Hilton; afterwards they are invited to meet with him in private. When the band were invited to attend a ten-day course in Wales, John eagerly signed up (top left). Two days in, they received the terrible news that Brian Epstein had been found dead at his London flat. It was assumed to be an accidental overdose and the coroner agreed, recording a verdict of accidental death. Outwardly, John showed little emotion and tried to remain positive but it must have been devastating for him. In an interview for *Rolling Stone* magazine in 1971, he admitted as much: "I knew we were in trouble then... I was scared."

Top right: A few weeks before the release of the Sgt. Pepper album, John unveils the psychedelic new paintwork on his Rolls-Royce Phantom V, painted with Romany scrolls and reminiscent of a gypsy caravan. The makeover cost £1,000 and took six weeks to complete.

> "We don't know what to say... he was one of us... so you can't pay a tribute in words".
> —**John on the death of Brian Epstein**

Magical Mystery Tour

Above: Earlier in the summer, The Beatles had been in the studio recording tracks for *Magical Mystery Tour*, a project championed by Paul. The idea was to make a free-form film with sketches and musical interludes based around a coach trip. Four days after Brian Epstein's death, The Beatles returned to Abbey Road studios to continue recording. Shooting began shortly after, with the crew, band and some members of the cast setting off in the *Magical Mystery Tour* bus from central London for an initial five-day stint in the West Country. On day two, the coach became stuck on a narrow bridge on its way to the next location of Widecombe Fair (above inset). Tempers frayed as it had to reverse and the Widecombe scenes were abandoned.

Opposite: John sports a fedora with feathers during filming.

Magical Mystery Tour received a critical mauling – the consensus was that it was a £40,000 home movie punctuated by some fine songs.

''I Am the Walrus'', Lennon's favourite Beatles' song, was a gem that had his unmistakable signature.

Reluctant Road Tripper

John pictured on location in Devon. In Plymouth (opposite) he signed autographs for fans and posed for photographers. A posse of journalists had pursued him and the rest of the band from London, bemused and intrigued by the whole project.

The *Magical Mystery Tour* experience did not prove to be an entirely happy one for John. He had traditionally had the final say in The Beatles' decision-making process, but now Paul was determined to exert executive control over the project, leading to frequent disagreements between the two of them, during both the location filming and the editing process. Afterwards, John expressed regret over the project, suggesting it was done simply to keep the fans happy. But most fans were sadly disappointed, believing – as did the majority of the critics – that the finished movie had suffered as a result of its haphazard production.

I am the Walrus

Left: The *Magical Mystery Tour* project was chaotic and beset with problems. Ten hours of footage was eventually edited down to a 55-minute TV film, shown in black and white on the BBC on Boxing Day. The film was slated universally by the press, the critic for the *Evening News* saying: "There was precious little magic and the only mystery was how the BBC came to buy it."

The soundtrack however, released in the UK as a six-song double EP and given the full album treatment in the United States, was more warmly received. John's "I Am the Walrus" was a substantial contribution; his final masterpiece of 1967 contained a heady mix of surrealist images intended as a dig at the pretentious intellectuals who read meaning into the lyrics that were never there. John is reported to have said, "Let them work that one out", referring to the line: "Semolina pilchards/Climbing up the Eiffel Tower".

Below and opposite: Shortly after Brian Epstein's death, John and George appeared on two editions of David Frost's new discussion show, *The Frost Programme*, where they talked about the relative virtues of LSD and Transcendental Meditation. The first programme also featured an interview with the Maharishi Mahesh Yogi. John and the others were understandably devastated by Brian's death; although he had had less contact with the Beatles since their decision to stop touring, he had been there almost right from the start, and had been an important friend as well as helping them to reach the dizzying heights of fame. Outwardly though, John showed little emotion – it was not the first time he had channelled his grief inwards. However, his newfound interest in Transcendental Meditation and Eastern philosophy undoubtedly helped him to cope, and he looked forward to travelling to India to continue his spiritual quest.

John's film premiere

This page and opposite top right: On October 18, the day after a memorial service was held in London in honour of Brian Epstein, John attends the London Pavilion for the world premiere of Dick Lester's *How I Won The War*, which he had filmed a year earlier. All of The Beatles were in attendance with their respective partners, but although John arrived with Cynthia on his arm, a mutual infatuation had been developing between him and Yoko Ono. Just days before, Yoko's latest exhibition *Yoko Plus Me*, had opened at the Lisson Gallery, with John's financial support. Cynthia could not fail to be aware of Yoko's existence, for the artist had bombarded John with a steady stream of letters and phone calls since they met, and on more than one occasion Yoko had turned up unannounced at their home. However, having confronted John about the matter, Cynthia seemed not to perceive this curious Japanese woman as a threat.

Opposite below: Earlier in the year, The Beatles had formed an umbrella company – The Beatles & Co. – to control their various business interests. The new company gave each Beatle five per cent ownership; a new corporation – Apple Corps – was established in January the following year and owned collectively by the four. It bound them together until 1977, which proved to be a costly mistake within a few years.

Opposite top left: John and Cynthia arrive for the opening of the Apple Boutique in Baker Street, London. Following Brian Epstein's death, The Beatles launched various enterprises, one of them being the Apple Boutique, a shop selling "beautiful things for beautiful people". Designed by The Fool, a Dutch collective, it was managed by a school friend of John's and Pattie Harrison's sister.

LONDON PAVILION PICCADILLY CIRCUS W.1

GALA PREMIERE
WEDNESDAY, 18th OCTOBER, 1967 at 8.0 for 8.30 p.m.

MICHAEL CRAWFORD   HOW I WON THE WAR   JOHN LENNON

ROY KINNEAR   LEE MONTAGUE   JACK MacGOWRAN

MICHAEL HORDERN   JACK HEDLEY   KARL MICHAEL VOGLER

EASTMAN COLOUR

DRESS CIRCLE   **ROW A**   **SEAT No.** 13

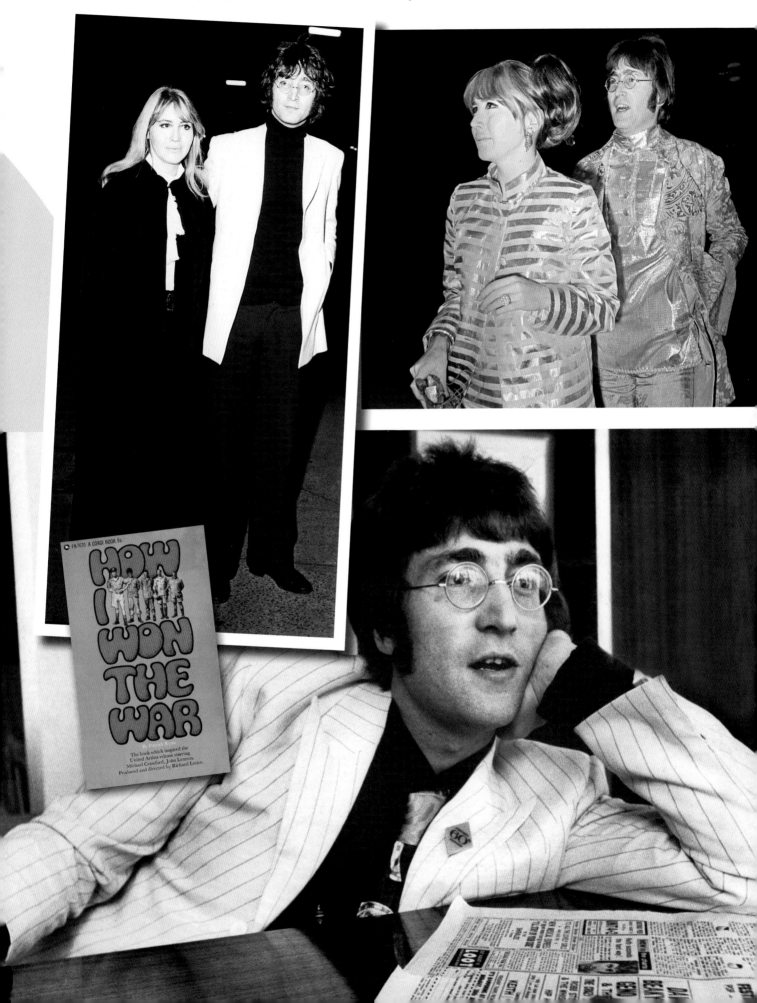

JOHN LENNON TIMELINE

1967

17 Feb UK single release of "Strawberry Fields Forever"/ "Penny Lane". It fails to reach the top of the chart - the first single not to do so since "Please, Please Me" reached No. 2 in January 1963.

26 May The Beatles' ground-breaking album *Sgt. Pepper's Lonely Hearts Club Band* is released ahead of the official date of 1 June.

25 Jun The Beatles perform "All You Need Is Love" on the world's first global satellite television link-up.

24 Jul John, Paul, George, Ringo and Brian Epstein sign a petition published in *The Times* calling for the legalization of marijuana.

24 Aug John, George and Paul, with wives and friends, attend a lecture given by the Maharishi Mahesh Yogi in London, travelling to a weekend seminar in North Wales the following day.

27 Aug Brian Epstein is found dead at home in bed, London.

11 Sept Shooting begins on The Beatles' next film, *Magical Mystery Tour*.

30 Sept John and George appear on ITV's *The Frost Programme* with the Maharishi.

11 Oct *Yoko Plus Me*, an exhibition at London's Lisson Art Gallery, is anonymously sponsored by John.

18 Oct *How I Won the War* premieres at the London Pavilion.

5 Dec John and George attend the opening party for The Beatles' Apple Boutique.

16 Dec John and George attend a UNICEF gala in Paris with the Maharishi.

26 Dec The BBC premieres *Magical Mystery Tour* (in black and white) to a great deal of public criticism.

Apple – conveying purity and simplicity – was the perfect logo for the new Beatles' enterprise. The retail experiment would fold after just eight months.

Launching the Apple Boutique

John had planned the launch of the boutique to be by invitation only, but in the event, it was overrun with gate-crashers. As he and Cynthia arrived, crowds surged in, reminding John of the "Beatlemania" days.

The premises did not have a licence, so apple juice instead of alcohol was the order of the day. As well and John and George, some celebrities attended, including Cilla Black, Twiggy, Eric Clapton and the critic and writer, Kenneth Tynan.

This page and opposite main image: The Apple Boutique proved to be a commercial failure and closed within eight months. Years later, John talked about it scathingly as a shop "...with all this junk and The Fool and all the stupid clothes and all that".

Opposite inset: John sponsored an exhibition by Jonathan Hague, with whom he had briefly attended art college in Liverpool.

Hello and goodbye

Above: A clown at the Apple Boutique launch party fails to impress or amuse John. He had apparently vetoed the use of the word "boutique" for the shop, but it had stuck.

Opposite: John and Cynthia leave the Apple Boutique launch party. The concept was that the shop sold everything; in fact, most of the stock consisted of fashion clothing and accessories. The business lost money at a worrying rate and when it closed in July 1968, The Beatles decided to give away the remaining stock – attracting massive crowds to the final days of the store.

Right: John in fancy dress at the *Magical Mystery Tour* launch party at the Lancaster Hotel, London, just before Christmas 1967. "Hello Goodbye" had been released in late November and reached No. 1 within two weeks. John's "I Am the Walrus" was the B-side and gave him the pleasure of seeing his composition occupy the top spot over Christmas.

CHAPTER SIX

1968

I'm so tired

At the beginning of 1968, Fred Lennon turned up at John's home in Weybridge again. He had met nineteen-year-old former student Pauline Jones, and they wanted to get married. Unfortunately, her mother was very much set against the idea, and had made her daughter a ward of court. John found a job for Pauline temporarily as his secretary, allowed her to stay in his home and later paid for their wedding in Scotland, which was out of the English court's jurisdiction. Later he bought the couple a house in Kew, and finally established a workable, if not close, relationship with his father.

In February John and Cynthia flew to the Himalayan retreat of the Maharishi Mahesh Yogi in India to attend a three-month course in Transcendental Meditation. They were accompanied by George and Pattie and the other two Beatles and their partners followed a few days later. Ringo and Maureen had had enough after less than two weeks, while Paul and Jane left after five. John and George stayed for almost two months, before becoming disillusioned with the Maharishi's character and methods – although not with his basic message.

Soon after their return to England, John and Paul went to New York for five days, where John took the opportunity to denounce the Maharishi, while appearing on NBC's *Tonight Show*. However, the reason for their trip was to announce the formation of Apple Corps Ltd. The new company was to have different divisions covering areas such as music, films, electronics, merchandise and the arts, and one of its functions was to invest funds to help creative people start out. This was supposed to be run on a business footing, so that at some point there would be a return on the investment. John and Paul took it all very seriously and went into Apple's offices every day to direct operations. However, since no one appeared to check whether funds going out would ever bring any sort of return, Apple soon became a source of easy money to anyone who knocked on the door. The company executives and staff also took full advantage of the situation, awarding themselves lavish salaries and large expense accounts. One employee later described working there as being "the longest cocktail party", but for some time neither John nor the others realized what was going on.

John was still fascinated with Yoko, who had written to him regularly while he was in India. In May, he invited her to his home while Cynthia was away on holiday and the two of them sat up all night experimenting with sounds and recording music and voices, and had then finally gone to bed. From that moment on it was inevitable that they would be together. Although Cynthia came home to find Yoko there, initially John refused to face up to the situation and make the break, so he and Cynthia carried on living together for another few weeks.

Cynthia soon left again for Italy on a prearranged holiday with Julian and her mother, and while she was away John and Yoko began to appear in public together. When they planted acorns in the grounds of Coventry Cathedral as part of the National Sculpture Exhibition, it could just have been seen as a natural progression of John's interest in art. The acorns

Opposite: John poses with Yoko and Julian.

were supposed to represent East and West, symbolizing the meeting of two different cultures. However, when they arrived hand-in-hand at the London premiere of *In His Own Write*, a play based on John's two books, there was no concealing the situation any longer and journalists had a field day. They called out to John, asking him where his wife was, and pictures of him and Yoko appeared in most of the national papers. Cynthia saw them in Italy and knew that her marriage was over; by the end of the year she and John were divorced.

Now John and Yoko were openly together, he became even more publicly involved with the art world. In July the first exhibition of his own work, *You Are Here*, opened in the Robert Fraser Gallery in central London. It consisted of a display of fifty charity collecting boxes and was dedicated to Yoko. Before the opening, he and Yoko, both dressed all in white, released 365 helium-filled balloons over London. Although Yoko was still married to American film director Anthony Cox, she was also now heading for divorce.

Despite his new interests, John still had commitments from the past to fulfil. The original deal that had been done with United Artists meant that one more Beatles film had to be made. None of them had been particularly interested in doing it, but they had agreed on a full-length animated film to be based on one of their earlier songs, which was two years in the making; *Yellow Submarine* was finally released in 1968. Although The Beatles had been consulted about the concept at the beginning, they had not been involved in developing the storyline and even the voice-overs were done by actors. However, they did write four new songs for the soundtrack and filmed a short cameo appearance, which was inserted near the end. The film was poorly distributed in Britain, but did extremely well in America and was very highly regarded by the critics – later it was often dubbed "the best film The Beatles never made". The group turned out in force for the London premiere of *Yellow Submarine* in July, and John was again accompanied by Yoko.

One unexpected advantage of The Beatles' long stay in India was that it had removed them from their usual environments and given both John and Paul ample time to write new songs – and George had also been hard at work. They had returned with enough material for a new album, and soon went into the studio to begin recording their double LP, *The Beatles* – later known as the *White Album* to distinguish it from the name of the band. However, problems quickly surfaced. John and Paul did not really like each other's new songs, while George felt his material was constantly being dismissed. On top of this, Yoko was now ever present in the studio, whispering to John, encouraging his

ideas – and actually daring to criticize and comment on the work in progress. Until then outsiders had been banned and wives and girlfriends had only been allowed to watch from the control room; the other Beatles bitterly resented Yoko's presence on the studio floor. The tension became so bad that Ringo, always the most easy-going of the four, walked out – technically becoming the first Beatle to leave the group, although he was talked into returning just over a week later.

Although it was common knowledge that The Beatles had experimented with drugs, as did many other well-known pop artists at the time, until now there had been no official move against any of them. In October that year, however, John and Yoko were awoken early in the morning by police with dogs at the door of the flat they shared in Montagu Square. After a thorough search, a small piece of cannabis was found and they were arrested and charged. John later maintained that it was a set-up – he had been tipped off by a journalist that the police were taking an interest and had cleaned the flat out, so he was sure the drugs had been planted. However, he pleaded guilty to protect Yoko – even though

he knew a conviction might cause problems if he wanted to visit America. He was fined £150 and ordered to pay twenty guineas costs.

By now Yoko was several months pregnant, with her baby due the following February. The announcement hastened John's divorce through the courts – until then he had been maintaining that he had not been unfaithful in an attempt to minimize the settlement due to Cynthia. Unfortunately, Yoko miscarried the following month; John stayed with her at the hospital, sleeping first in the next bed and then on the floor, but refusing to leave her side.

At the end of November, John and Yoko released their first album together, *Unfinished Music No. 1: Two Virgins*, a collection of strange sounds and musical effects, most of which had been recorded back in May during that first evening together at John's house in Weybridge. When John decided the two of them should be photographed naked for the front and back of the sleeve, EMI declined to distribute the record and it was released through Apple. It was not only panned by the critics but also a commercial failure on both sides of the Atlantic – thousands of copies were impounded and confiscated by Customs as indecent. John was not concerned – the record had been released as a statement rather than as a commercial venture.

In December John and Yoko both appeared on stage at the Royal Albert Hall concealed in a large white bag for *Alchemical Wedding*, the underground art world's Christmas party; they distributed presents together at the Apple Christmas party, John dressed as Father Christmas and Yoko as Mother Christmas. John was rapidly losing interest in doing anything with The Beatles – he wanted to move forward artistically with Yoko. However, something urgently needed to be done about Apple Corps, which had spent more than £1 million but made nothing in return. The boutique in Baker Street had closed; when all the left-over stock was given away it was the first time crowds fought to get into the store. The other Beatles still seemed unaware of the problem but, despite his laid-back demeanour, John had always had a surprisingly sharp business brain and he soon blew the whistle on what was going on.

Above: John, Yoko and Paul arrive at the London Pavillion for the premiere of Yellow Submarine.

Opposite: John and Yoko at the opening of John's first art exhibition *You Are Here* in July 1968 at the Robert Fraser Gallery in London. Yoko's own work was also on display.

Promoting Apple Corps

Top right: John and Cynthia at a party at the Revolution nightclub in London. Sitting next to John is Alexis Mardas; "Magic Alex", as Lennon called him, was influential in persuading The Beatles to go to Greece the previous year on a potential island-buying trip.

Below and bottom: After launching the Apple Boutique, The Beatles established Apple Publishing, the precursor to the Apple record label; their first signing was Grapefruit. John and the rest of the band, together with Cilla Black, Brian Jones and Donovan, attended a press conference for the release of the newcomers' first song, "Dear Delilah". Apple Records went on to sign notable artists including James Taylor, Billy Preston and Mary Hopkin.

Opposite inset: John with the Maharishi. In the middle of February, John and the other Beatles flew to India to spend time at the Yogi's retreat in Rishikesh. The spiritual retreat, postponed from the previous year, was intended to further their Transcendental Meditation studies. John and George were the most enthusiastic and committed of the four; Ringo and Paul were more open-minded, although Ringo lasted only two weeks before heading home with Maureen, complaining the food disagreed with him. Paul and Jane Asher followed a few weeks later.

Two months into the stay in Rishikesh, rumours began circulating about the Maharishi's less than spiritual practices and a disillusioned John returned to England after confronting him. Later, he denounced the Maharishi in song, substituting the Yogi's name with "Sexy Sadie" and the lines "…what have you done/ You made a fool of everyone", referring to his alleged sexual advances towards the actress Mia Farrow; the track was included on the *White Album* released later in the year.

When the Maharishi asked why he was leaving so soon, John replied, "If you're so cosmic, you'll know why".

Above: Within a month of returning to the UK from Rishikesh, John flies to New York with Paul to unveil plans and promote Apple Corps, the umbrella organization for all The Beatles' business ventures.

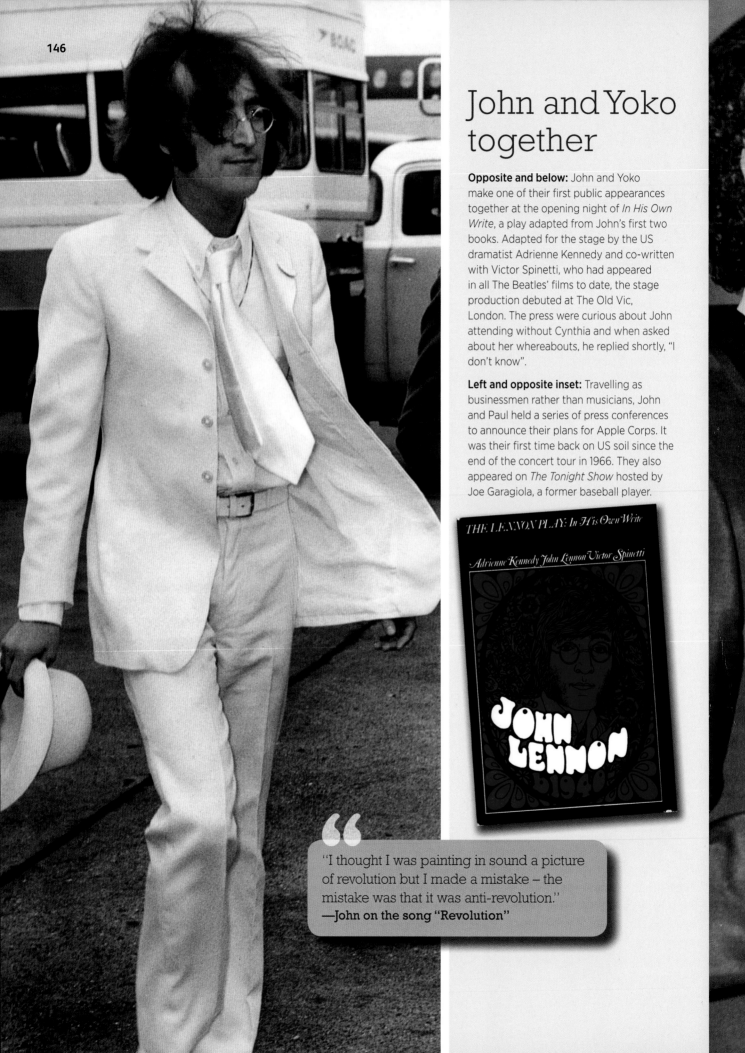

John and Yoko together

Opposite and below: John and Yoko make one of their first public appearances together at the opening night of *In His Own Write*, a play adapted from John's first two books. Adapted for the stage by the US dramatist Adrienne Kennedy and co-written with Victor Spinetti, who had appeared in all The Beatles' films to date, the stage production debuted at The Old Vic, London. The press were curious about John attending without Cynthia and when asked about her whereabouts, he replied shortly, "I don't know".

Left and opposite inset: Travelling as businessmen rather than musicians, John and Paul held a series of press conferences to announce their plans for Apple Corps. It was their first time back on US soil since the end of the concert tour in 1966. They also appeared on *The Tonight Show* hosted by Joe Garagiola, a former baseball player.

THE LENNON PLAY: *In His Own Write*

Adrienne Kennedy John Lennon Victor Spinetti

JOHN LENNON

"I thought I was painting in sound a picture of revolution but I made a mistake – the mistake was that it was anti-revolution."
—**John on the song "Revolution"**

John in love

Left: John signing autographs at the premiere of *In His Own Write*. When interviewed for BBC2's art programme *Release*, he revealed how emotional he had been about seeing the play in rehearsal for the first time. It had a mixed reception from the critics.

Opposite inset: Yoko Ono sitting on a draped lion in Trafalgar Square, part of her "wrapping event" exhibit of 1966; she was photographed by her then husband, the US director, Anthony Cox.

Below and opposite: John and Yoko had appeared in public together for the first time in June, planting acorns for peace at Coventry Cathedral. At the beginning of July, they attend the opening of his first art exhibition *You Are Here* at the Robert Fraser Gallery in Mayfair. They both wore white to match the gallery's décor and 365 white helium-filled balloons were released into the London skies. John is said to have publicly declared his love for Yoko at the venue; at the time she was still married to her second husband, Anthony Cox. Lennon's divorce from Cynthia was another four months away.

> "I knew there was no way I could ever fight the unity of mind and body they had with each other…Yoko did not take John away from me because he had never really been mine." —Cynthia Lennon

JOHN LENNON TIMELINE

1968

5 Jan John is visited at his Weybridge home by his father, who seeks John's blessing in marrying nineteen-year-old Pauline Jones.

25 Jan John and George attend an Ossie Clark fashion show in London. George's wife Pattie is among the models.

15 Feb John, Cynthia, George and Pattie fly to Rishikesh in India to study meditation with the Maharishi Mahesh Yogi.

12 Apr John, Cynthia, George and Pattie arrive back in London.

11 May John and Paul go to New York for five days, where they announce the establishment of their Apple business venture.

14 May John denounces the Maharishi on NBC's *The Tonight Show* and announces the formation of Apple Corps.

22 May John and Yoko Ono appear together in public for the first time, attending a party and press conference for another Apple Boutique.

15 Jun John and Yoko participate in the National Sculpture Exhibition by planting two acorns outside Coventry Cathedral; it marks their first "event".

18 Jun John attends the opening of *In His Own Write* with Yoko. The play had been adapted by actor and friend Victor Spinetti from John's two books.

21 Jun Apple Corps buys premises on Savile Row, London.

1 Jul *You Are Here*, John's first art exhibition, opens in London with the release of 365 balloons.

22 Aug Cynthia sues John for divorce, on the grounds of his affair with Yoko Ono.

The Ultimate Trip

Since their first meeting in 1966, Yoko Ono had been writing to John on a regular basis, and indeed, he received almost daily missives from her while in India. Cynthia knew of her existence but had been persuaded by John that she was just another obsessed fan.

While Cynthia was on holiday in Greece, John invited Yoko to Kenwood, where they recorded *Two Virgins*, a collection of avant-garde musical recordings.

On her return, Cynthia found John and Yoko together at Kenwood and knew that her marriage was over. John described Yoko as "the ultimate trip" He was convinced that he had found "the one", the intellectual and creative equal who had awoken him from his creative slumbers — but also someone he could completely relax with, remarking that he could happily take her to the pub like an old friend from Liverpool. Yoko also undoubtedly represented an escape for John: from his marriage; from Kenwood; perhaps, he hoped, even from fame, money, and The Beatles. However, by now they were both regularly using heroin.

He later said that meeting her was like meeting your first woman – "Once I found THE woman, the boys became of no interest".

JOHN LENNON TIMELINE

1968

18 Oct A police raid takes place at 34 Montagu Square, London, a flat owned by Ringo, where John and Yoko are staying. The pair are charged with obstructing the police and with possession of cannabis.

25 Oct John and Yoko announce that Yoko is pregnant, the child is expected in February the following year.

8 Nov John and Cynthia are divorced.

21 Nov Yoko miscarries her child and John stays with her at Queen Charlotte's Maternity Hospital, Hammersmith, London.

22 Nov "The White Album"—its official title is the decidedly simple The Beatles—is released

28 Nov John pleads guilty to possession of cannabis, while charges against Yoko are dropped. John is fined £150 and twenty guineas costs. Both are found not guilty of obstruction.

29 Nov John and Yoko's first album, *Unfinished Music No 1: Two Virgins*, sees its UK release.

10 Dec John's home, Kenwood, is put up for sale.

11 Dec John takes part in the Rolling Stones' *Rock and Roll Circus*, which remains uncompleted.

18 Dec John and Yoko appear inside a white bag at the Royal Albert Hall, London, as part of *Alchemical Wedding*, a party hosted by the underground art movement.

23 Dec Apple holds its Christmas party at Savile Row, where John and Yoko hand out gifts dressed as Father and Mother Christmas.

> "When I met Yoko is when you meet your first woman and you leave the guys at the bar, and you don't play football any more…Once I found the woman, the boys became of no interest whatsoever, other than they were like old friends." —**John**

John's changing look

Top right: John's Tussauds' waxwork – the fifth makeover for The Beatles – with new clothing and hairstyles to keep up with their changing images.

Middle right: John and Paul at the London premiere of *Yellow Submarine* at the London Pavilion. Their contractual obligations meant that the boys had to release another feature film in 1968. A full-length animation, *Yellow Submarine* had minimal production involvement from The Beatles apart from a short live-action sequence filmed at Twickenham Studios in January. The voices for their cartoon alter egos were provided by actors. The soundtrack album, issued in January 1969, comprised the title track, orchestral music provided by George Martin and four new Beatles songs as well as John's "All You Need is Love".

Below right and Opposite: John and Yoko were becoming increasingly inseparable. He had angered the other Beatles by inviting her into the studio while the band were recording the *White Album*, even affording her a microphone to make comments. John later felt that the rest of the band's animosity towards Yoko led to his composition, "Revolution", released as a B-side to Paul's "Hey Jude". He commented that her presence had helped him to recapture his creativity: "... after lying fallow for a couple of years... it upset the apple cart. I was awake again and they weren't used to it." Symbolic of his total commitment to their relationship, John had also introduced Yoko to his Aunt Mimi, who had raised him as a child.

Yoko Ono

Yoko Ono was born into a prosperous Tokyo banking family on 18 February 1933. Her formative years were spent commuting between Japan and America, where her father worked, and at the end of World War II the family relocated to the US. They settled in the well-heeled Scarsdale district of New York and Yoko attended Harvard and Sarah Lawrence School, where Linda Eastman would also study. Against her family's wishes she married Japanese musician Toshi Ichyanagi, an ill-starred match that foundered long before the couple's 1962 divorce. By then she had already met her second husband, New York musician and film producer Anthony Cox, with whom she had a daughter, Kyoko, born 8 August 1963. Over the next three years Yoko made a name for herself as an avant-garde artist. She published *Grapefruit*, a book filled with Zen-like instructions, and her conceptual artwork included a forerunner to bagism.

In September 1966 Yoko and Cox came to London to further her career, which needed new sponsorship. She attended a symposium called The Destruction of Art and naturally fell into the orbit of Barry Miles, Peter Asher and John Dunbar, who ran Indica Gallery and were acquainted with The Beatles. John met Yoko on 9 November 1966, when he attended her Indica exhibition titled *Unfinished Paintings and Objects*. Exhibits such as a card inviting the reader to "Breathe" appealed to John's wry sense of humour.

Eighteen months passed before Yoko's tenacious pursuit of John bore fruit. In that time the self-styled "High Priestess of the Happening" featured regularly in the newspaper columns, which reported on events such as wrapping the Trafalgar Square lions with paper. Yoko regularly turned up uninvited at Kenwood and in May 1968, with Cynthia out of the country, John yielded to her enigmatic charms. The pair made experimental tapes that would eventually be released as *Two Virgins*. They also became lovers. The couple collaborated on a number of projects, while Yoko's attendance at Abbey Road during Beatles recording sessions caused resentment, exacerbating existing tensions.

John and Yoko married in Gibraltar on 20 March 1969, inviting the world's press to their honeymoon "Bed-In for Peace". They moved to New York after The Beatles disbanded and, following an eighteen-month estrangement, when John co-habited with personal assistant May Pang, the couple reconciled in 1975. Sean Taro Ono Lennon was born on 9 October that year. Over the next five years Yoko showed considerable business acumen, quadrupling their fortune while John took on the role of house-husband. He had just returned to the creative arena with *Double Fantasy* when he was gunned down on 8 December 1980. Since then, Yoko has released a number of John's works, and many others in her own right. She has attended countless dedication ceremonies, including the inauguration of the Strawberry Fields memorial in Central Park, near the Dakota building apartment they shared.

"Our minds met on the music on the record, and our bodies met on the cover of the record."
—John on *Two Virgins*

"She makes music like you've never heard on earth… it's as important as anything we ever did."
—John on Yoko's musical ability in Nov 1968

Charged with possession

This page and opposite: By the autumn of 1968, John and Yoko were living at Ringo's Montagu Square flat. Early on October 18, the flat was raided by the drug squad. John had been warned by a journalist that the raid was likely, and the couple had cleaned the flat of any traces of drugs. However, the police found 219 grains of cannabis resin on the premises.

The pair were arrested and charged with possession as well as obstructing the police in the execution of a search warrant. They appeared at Marylebone Magistrates Court the following day, where they were remanded on bail to appear again at the end of November.

John took the rap and pleaded guilty. Yoko had recently suffered a late miscarriage – they had announced the pregnancy only the month before – and they were also worried that if they fought the charges and lost, she could be deported from the UK.

John fined

Left: The obstruction charge was quashed and John was fined £150 for the cannabis possession. The fall-out from the case lasted well into the next decade, when Lennon's conviction was used as a key factor in denying him a Green Card residency permit in the US.

Below and opposite: In early December John, Yoko and Julian join Brian Jones and the rest of the Rolling Stones as guests on the Stones' planned television special, *The Rolling Stones Rock and Roll Circus*. The end of 1968 was an important period for John; he and Cynthia were divorced in early November, just prior to the release of John and Yoko's LP, *Unfinished Music No. 1: Two Virgins*, with its controversial cover depicting John and Yoko naked. At the end of the month, The Beatles' eponymous double album, which became better known as the *White Album*, was also released.

> "
>
> "The Beatles could have afforded to put out the slow, understandable version of "Revolution" as a single… but because they were upset over the Yoko thing and the fact that I was becoming as creative and dominating as I was in the early days – after lying fallow for a couple of years – it upset the applecart. I was awake again and they weren't used to it."—**John**

CHAPTER SEVEN

1969

Love is old, love is new

At the beginning of January, The Beatles assembled at Twickenham Studios to be filmed rehearsing, as part of a documentary that was to show them preparing for either a television broadcast or a concert. Almost immediately the tensions between them surfaced – they are clearly apparent in the final film, *Let It Be*. This time George walked out and although he was persuaded to return, the idea of a concert was shelved. When The Beatles played live at the end of January on the roof of the Apple building, which was filmed for *Let It Be*, it was the last time they performed together as a group. Meanwhile, they went back to the studio to record an LP, but although the final tapes were not up to their usual high standard, none of them could face further work on it. Instead they decided to start afresh – and this time produced *Abbey Road*, one of their best LPs.

John had been concerned about the state of Apple Corps for some time, but early that year he went public, telling *Disc and Music Echo* that he and the others had made a big mistake with Apple, and that they now realized they were not businessmen. He went on to say, "…if it carries on like this all of us will be broke in the next six months". Paul was furious that John had spoken to the press, although he accepted that there were problems that needed to be addressed. However, the four of them could not all agree on who should be appointed to come in and sort things out. John and Yoko wanted Allen Klein, a tough New York show-business lawyer, who had been introduced to them by The Rolling Stones, and they eventually convinced George and Ringo. Paul didn't trust Klein and wanted the New York firm of Eastman & Eastman – run by his girlfriend Linda's father and brother – but John and the others felt the Eastmans would only be looking out for Paul's best interests. John and Yoko prevailed and Klein's company, ABKCO, was appointed – it was the first time The Beatles had done anything without all four members being in agreement.

Another business problem now came to a head – the group lost their controlling interest in Brian Epstein's old company, NEMS, and in Northern Songs, the company that published their songs. This meant they no longer owned the rights to any of their compositions and valuable royalties were going to other people. Klein failed to stop it happening – although he did achieve a much better royalty deal from EMI for the group's American sales.

Yoko's divorce from Anthony Cox had come through in February and she and John were finally able to marry in March. At the time they were based in Paris, but decided to charter a plane and fly to Gibraltar to get married at the British Consulate. They both wore white for the wedding – as John said, they were "tremendous romantics". They spent just over an hour in Gibraltar, before flying back to Paris, but told the press to look out for another "happening". Journalists did not have long to wait – a few days later the happy couple took over the presidential suite at the Amsterdam Hilton and announced they were planning to stay in bed together for seven days. They invited the press, and journalists from around the world turned up to find John and Yoko dressed in white and surrounded by flowers, with

---

Opposite: John at *The Rolling Stones Rock and Roll Circus*, filmed in London, December 1968.

notices pinned up saying "Bed Peace" and "Hair Peace". John urged everyone to stay in bed and grow their hair, instead of being violent. It became the first of several "bed-ins" for peace, and they also came up with several other ideas to catch the attention of the press.

At the end of March their film *Rape* was premiered on Austrian television, and at a brief press conference in Vienna John and Yoko publicly launched "bagism", another manifestation of their peace campaign. They appeared on stage together inside a large white bag and refused to emerge, although they happily answered questions. One benefit of "bagism", John explained, was that no one could be distracted from their message by the colour of their skin, or the length of their hair.

As John became more involved with Yoko, he found that he developed different ideas about many things. She pointed out how unfair it was that she had had to change her name when they married, so he decided to change his too. At an official ceremony on the roof of the Apple building, he became John Ono Lennon – although he never entirely managed to get rid of his original middle name, Winston, legally. The two of them soon bought a home together – Tittenhurst Park, where the last photograph of all four Beatles together was taken later that year.

Although he was no longer interested in performing with The Beatles, John had by no means given up music. He released a second LP with Yoko, *Unfinished Music No. 2: Life with the Lions*. Musically it was not a great success, but that was not the point – he just wanted to continue experimenting and push the boundaries even further.

Although John's application for a US visa had been rejected because of his 1968 drugs conviction, Canada proved more welcoming and another bed-in for peace was staged at a hotel in Montreal. While there, a makeshift group of friends and acquaintances – which was christened the Plastic Ono Band – recorded a new song John had written, "Give Peace a Chance". It was one of his most successful compositions and went on to become the anthem for the peace movement.

Despite the excitement of his new life, John felt guilty about abandoning Julian and continued to see him regularly, just as Yoko tried to spend time with Kyoko. In July they took both children for a weekend in Scotland, where John hired a car. He was not a good driver and badly misjudged a bend rolling off the road into a ditch; he and Yoko were badly cut, Kyoko was slightly injured and Julian suffered from shock. They were taken to the local hospital where John, Yoko and Kyoko all had to have stitches and were kept in for several days. Julian was fine, but Cynthia quickly arrived to collect him and take him back to London.

Soon afterwards John and Yoko were supposed to be appearing at the launch of the Plastic Ono Band in London, but since they were still in hospital their stand-ins were a pair of Perspex tubes fitted with microphones, tape recorders and amplifiers. John felt it was very symbolic, showing the world that the Plastic Ono Band was a conceptual band with no actual members. However, they soon began releasing records – beginning with John's first solo single, "Give Peace a Chance". In September, the Plastic Ono Band was invited to perform at a concert in Toronto. John called up several old friends, including Eric Clapton and Klaus Voormann, just the night before; they rehearsed on the plane on the way over. John loved this kind of spontaneity, even if the final result was rather raw – he found the endless polishing to perfection done on The Beatles' songs laborious and boring. On the way to Toronto John decided finally that he wanted to quit The Beatles and told his companions. He later told Klein as well, but was persuaded to keep it quiet for the moment because negotiations with EMI to achieve an increased offer were at a delicate stage.

The peace campaign was doing well, but John decided that it needed an extra push and even more publicity. He sent his chauffeur to "borrow" his MBE back from Mimi – who was horrified to read in the papers the following day that he had returned it to the Queen. He enclosed a note, explaining that he was protesting against Britain's involvement in Biafra, America's involvement in Vietnam and against his current record slipping down the charts. He later explained to the press that he had always felt uncomfortable about accepting the honour, but that he had done so because it was expected of a Beatle. Now he was rejecting it to draw attention to the peace campaign – and the reference to his record was a joke, so the Queen wouldn't think his letter was from "some boring colonel".

Before the end of the year he and Yoko were to take up yet another cause – they were introduced to the parents of James Hanratty, a convicted murderer who had been hanged in Britain in 1962. They became convinced of his innocence and began to take every opportunity to demonstrate on his behalf.

At the end of one of the most eventful years in his life, John felt he was finally beginning to get through to people. A poll in *Disc and Music Echo* not only named him the most popular Beatle, but revealed most readers were coming round to his views. Even the mainstream media had stopped treating him as if he were a joke – at the end of December he was featured in *Man of the Decade,* a three-part programme on ITV, along with John F. Kennedy and Mao Tse Tung.

Above: John and Yoko leave Heathrow Airport for Toronto to continue their peace campaign. They had expressed the hope that it would spell the beginning of "Year One AP (After Peace)".

John had broken a taboo inviting Yoko into the studio while The Beatles were recording the *White Album*.

Back in the studio

This page: Filming began for what was eventually titled *Let It Be* at the Twickenham Studios at the beginning of 1969. Despite producing *A Hard Day's Night*, *Help!* and *Yellow Submarine*, The Beatles were still obliged to produce a further movie for United Artists. The idea was to make a film of the band recording and rehearsing songs for an album, at the time called *Get Back*, at both the Twickenham and Apple studios, with a view to a televised performance. But the tensions were there from the beginning. John saw it as a Paul-led project and resented the loss of control; he was taking heroin and high most of the time; added to that he wanted to be with Yoko rather than the band. The following year he remembered it as being a "dreadful, dreadful feeling in Twickenham Studios and being filmed all the time"; George Martin concurred, calling it "a miserable experience". By day four, George Harrison had had enough and walked out on the band; he only agreed to return if recording moved to the Apple Studio in central London, which it was. Talk of a TV special was dropped and the filming would be The Beatles recording for a new album.

Opposite: John was not only invited to the filming of *The Rolling Stones Rock and Roll Circus* as an audience member (December 1968), but also as an active participant. He performed "Yer Blues", with a backing group, The Dirty Mac, consisting of Keith Richards, Eric Clapton, and Mitch Mitchell. As if to highlight the fractured state of The Beatles at this time, it was the first occasion that John had performed publicly without the rest of the group. Despite this Paul was pressing for the band to return to live performances as soon as possible.

"If there is still any doubt that Lennon and McCartney are the greatest songwriters since Schubert, then... [the album, The Beatles]...should surely see the last vestiges of cultural snobbery and bourgeois prejudice swept away in a deluge of joyful music making..." —Tony Palmer, *The Observer*

Final public performance

Opposite and above: The four weeks of filming culminated in an impromptu, rooftop, live performance on the Apple building in Central London. Low-key enough to ensure George and Ringo were on board, it had the joys of a concert performance without the hassle. The 42-minute set began around midday and attracted the attention of workers from nearby offices and shops out on their lunchbreak. A cold and blustery day, film of the event shows John wearing Yoko's fur coat and Ringo in Maureen's red mac. Billy Preston, who had been brought in a week earlier for his calming influence on the recording sessions as much as his musicianship, played organ alongside The Beatles. The set included "Get Back", released as a single the following April.

The performance was eventually shut down by the police, who had received complaints about the noise. As the curtain came down on The Beatles' final public performance, John stepped up to the microphone to say, "I'd like to say thanks on behalf of the group and ourselves and I hope we passed the audition". The comment was included at the end of the "Get Back" single and on the *Let It Be* album.

Right and opposite inset: The euphoria of the rooftop concert was short-lived – John and the other Beatles were ready to depart in different directions to pursue solo projects. However, there was one issue that they all agreed needed to be addressed: the parlous financial state of Apple Corps. John and Paul clashed over the solution: McCartney pushed for his future father-in-law's firm to represent the group, while John favoured Allen Klein who had an impressive track record in the entertainment industry. George and Ringo went along with John's plan and Paul was outvoted at a board meeting; the rift between the two was becoming wider.

> "I'd like to say 'thank you' on behalf of the group and ourselves and I hope we passed the audition."
> —John, closing line of The Beatles' rooftop concert, 30 January 1969

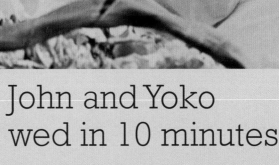

Yoko gets her man in just three minutes

From Daily Mail Correspondent GIBRALTAR, Thursday

JAPANESE actress Yoko Ono, 34, took Beatle John Lennon, MBE, for her third husband to-day — in three minutes flat.

Their marriage, behind the locked doors of Gibraltar's back - street register office, was sealed just after 9 a.m.

An hour later they were back aboard the chartered jet which had flown them to the Rock from Paris, where they will spend their honeymoon.

Mr Lennon, 28—whose first marriage was dissolved last year—told reporters: 'We want some peace and quiet.'

Miss Ono, previously married to a Japanese composer and then to American film producer Anthony Cox, by whom she has a six-year-old daughter, said nothing.

The build-up to the wedding —the second for a Beatle in eight days—began at Gibraltar Airport at 8.30 when their plane touched down.

With their two witnesses, Peter Brown, the Beatles' personal assistant, and photo-

After the wedding—Mr and Mrs Lennon.

grapher David Nutter, they took a car to the register office.

There, the registrar, Mr Cecil Wheeler, performed the special licence ceremony.

The bride and groom both wore white, including white tennis shoes.

Back in Paris, Mr Lennon said that he had not told the other Beatles: 'We never tell each other what we are doing. They are a loud-mouthed lot, like everybody else, you know.'

Before we went to his hotel he told reporters: 'I may have a big surprise for you on Monday.' But he gave no details.

John and Yoko wed in 10 minutes

Above and opposite: Yoko Ono's divorce from Tony Cox came during the *Get Back* sessions and in mid-March, she and John flew to Gibraltar – via Paris – where they were married in a 10-minute ceremony at the British Consulate. Dressed all in white, they immediately flew back to Paris for a few days' honeymooning. Then it was on to Amsterdam, courting publicity and controversy by staging a week-long "bed-in" at the Hilton Hotel. Here, they launched a peace campaign to the world's press, espousing the message: "stay in bed and grow your hair" as part of their anti-war stance.

Their third LP, *Wedding Album*, commemorating their wedding, was released towards the end of the year. A series of experimental recordings, it consisted of just two tracks: "John and Yoko" and "Amsterdam".

John's avant-garde leanings were becoming more apparent as his relationship with Yoko strengthened. His anti-war stance, particularly against the US involvement in Vietnam and the British reaction to the Biafran war in Nigeria, was more overt. Many thought the bed-in nothing more than a publicity stunt but Lennon as a political activist and humanitarian campaigner was now revealed.

> "Seems a bit silly to be in America and none of them mention Vietnam as if nothing was happening."—**John, during the 1966 tour of North America**

> "If everyone demanded peace instead of another TV set, we'd have peace".
> —**John, during the bed-in, Montreal**

Bagism

Although John had always been independent, freethinking, and outspoken, he had tended to suppress his more controversial or outlandish views – largely at the request of Brian Epstein, who had wished to present a carefully manicured image of his boys to the world's press. However, with Epstein's passing, and emboldened by Yoko, John no longer tried to bite his tongue or to suppress his avant-garde leanings. Some members of the press and public, and even close friends, began to wonder if he was simply courting attention, or had perhaps begun to lose his mind.

Opposite: Newly married John and Yoko shopping in a Paris flea market days after their return from Gibraltar.

This page: At the end of the week-long Amsterdam bed-in, the couple fly to Vienna for the premiere of their film *Rape*. A documentary about the effects of media intrusion, the film showed a girl being pursued by a camera crew. Following the screening, John and Yoko held a press conference inside a white bag at their hotel; this was their first revelation of the idea of "Bagism" – a form of total communication without visual prejudices.

Plant an acorn for peace

Above and opposite: On their return from their lightning trip to Vienna, John and Yoko arrive in London, where they attend a press conference, stating that they intended to send a pair of acorns to every world leader, thus encouraging them to plant trees rather than drop bombs. The previous June, John and Yoko had each planted an acorn outside Coventry Cathedral as part of a National Sculpture Exhibition. Following the press conference, John and Yoko made a live appearance on the *Today* programme on Thames Television, which was hosted by Eamonn Andrews. As in Vienna, they were interviewed inside a large, white sack, and once again promoted the idea of world peace and their concept of "bagism." However, on this occasion, perhaps because it was April Fool's Day, they managed to persuade the interviewer to join them in their bag.

"Imagine if the whole world stayed in bed. There'd be peace for a week and they might get to feel what it was like. The tension would be released".
—John and Yoko at Apple's London office on 8 May 1969 interviewed by David Wigg

Inseparable johnandyoko

By now, johnandyoko had become inseparable – they were rarely seen apart in public. She had replaced The Beatles in his life, for which he was thankful as it distracted him from the ongoing trials and tribulations surrounding the band's finances, as well as the increasingly tense relationships between the four.

In April John had formally changed his middle name by deed poll from Winston to Ono.

> "We were trying to sell peace like a product… the only way to get people aware that peace is possible…so advertise yourself that you're for peace, if you believe it."
> —Interview on the *David Frost Show*
> 14 June 1969

All we are saying...

After spending some time in London, John, Yoko and Kyoko flew to the Bahamas, where John hoped to stage another bed-in. It turned out to be less than ideal – the heat and humidity didn't lend itself to staying in bed for a week – and so they decamped to Montreal, where they staged the event at the Queen Elizabeth Hotel. The anthemic "Give Peace a Chance" was recorded at this time. Written by John and performed with Yoko, it was still credited to Lennon-McCartney. John later admitted his regret at this, saying he felt "guilty enough to give McCartney credit as co-writer of my first independent single instead of giving it to Yoko, who had actually written it with me".

Opposite and above: Yoko's daughter, Kyoko Cox, flies into Britain in May. The five-year-old was the daughter from Ono's marriage to Tony Cox, from whom she had been divorced the previous February.

Right: While in London Kyoko visits the Apple offices with her mother and John. John was spending more and more time at the Apple HQ trying to resolve The Beatles' financial and legal disputes, including the ownership of Northern Songs, the publishing company that owned the copyright to the Lennon-McCartney catalogue. Allen Klein had stripped away much of the dead wood in Apple Corps but in the end had failed to gain control of Northern Songs when Dick James (who co-founded it with Brian Epstein) had sold his shares in the company without offering The Beatles first refusal. John's expletive-ridden outburst at the eleventh hour of negotiations had not helped matters and the media tycoon Lew Grade took control.

66

"By the time we made *Abbey Road*, John and I were openly critical of each other's music and I felt John wasn't much interested in performing anything he hadn't written himself."—**Paul**

Forming the Plastic Ono Band

Left: While on holiday in Scotland at the beginning of July, John – with Yoko, Kyoko and Julian Lennon in the vehicle – crashed his car, driving into a roadside ditch. Julian was treated for shock and collected by a less-than-happy Cynthia the following day; the others all sustained facial injuries and received stitches. With John kept in hospital for five days, it meant they had to miss the launch of the Plastic Ono Band; it also delayed his return to London and his joining The Beatles for recording sessions for *Abbey Road*.

Opposite top left: At the very end of August, John, George and Ringo and their respective partners attend the Isle of Wight Festival to see Bob Dylan perform. The following day, Dylan visited John and Yoko at their new home, Tittenhurst Park, where John tried to persuade him to record "Cold Turkey". It was the second non-Beatle single he had written and was subsequently released under the Plastic Ono Band banner.

Opposite below right and left: Bagism was created by John and Yoko and formed part of their peace campaign. Promoted as a form of total communication, it espoused the idea that by covering the body of the person speaking, the listener could only hear the message and not be swayed by stereotypes or prejudices.

Opposite above right: Yoko in a contemplative pose. She was a controversial figure in the world of The Beatles and many felt that she contributed to the band's break-up.

66

"I thought it would be good to go out – the shitty version – because it would break The Beatles. It would break the myth: 'That's us with no trousers on and no glossy paint over the cover and no sort of hope'… but that didn't happen. We ended up making *Abbey Road* quickly and putting out something slick to preserve the myth."—**John on the subject of the *Get Back* recordings.** *Rolling Stone* 1971

"Paul was telling me the other day that he and I used to have rows about who was the leader. I can't remember them, it had stopped mattering by then. I wasn't so determined to be the leader at all costs. If I did argue, it was just out of pride. All the arguments were just trivial, mainly because we were irritable with working so hard. We were just kids."
—John

Recording
Abbey Road

This spread: A few days after returning from Scotland, John (along with Yoko) joined the rest of the band at the Abbey Road studios to begin in earnest recording for the forthcoming album. The sessions were not plain sailing; there was enough discontent and mistrust amongst the band to show that the writing was on the wall for their future together. Despite this, *Abbey Road* was well received by fans and gave the impression that the group had pulled together to create a fine collection of songs. In reality, after the basic rhythm had been laid down, harmonies were recorded individually. As had become the norm, John insisted Yoko was present during the sessions; as she had been prescribed bed-rest after the car accident, he had a bed installed in the studio so that she could attend.

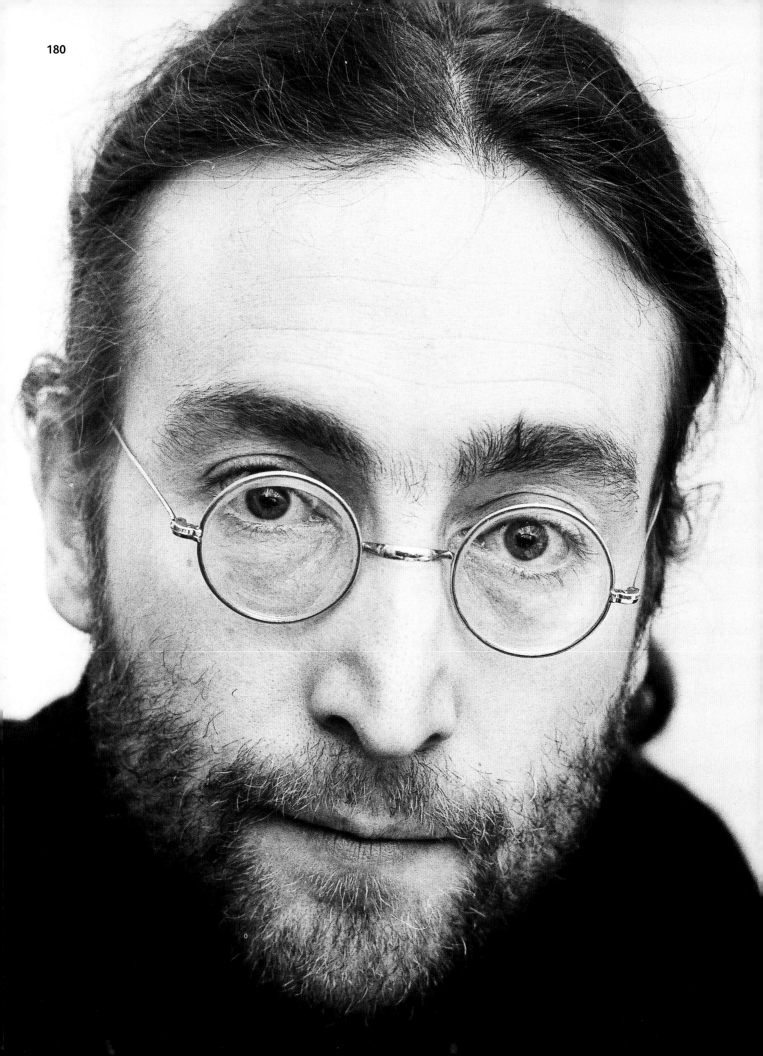

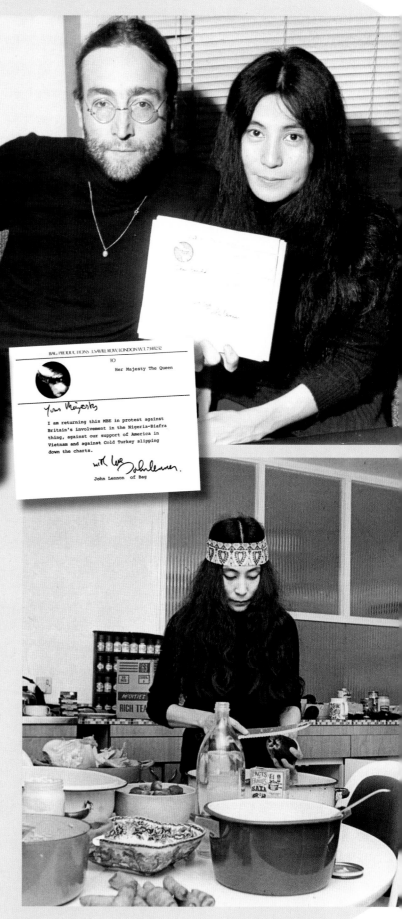

> "John Lennon has said that *Abbey Road* is an attempt to get away from experimentation and back to genuine rock 'n' roll. When one is as inventive as The Beatles, to try non-experimentation is a forlorn hope." —**William Mann,** *The Times*

BAG PRODUCTIONS, 3 SAVILE ROW, LONDON W.1, 734 82 12

TO
Her Majesty The Queen

Your Majesty

I am returning this MBE in protest against
Britain's involvement in the Nigeria-Biafra
thing, against our support of America in
Vietnam and against Cold Turkey slipping
down the charts.

with love John Lennon.

John Lennon of Bag

John's decision

Almost a month after completion of *Abbey Road*, John broke the news to the others that he was leaving The Beatles. He had made the decision a week earlier as he travelled to the Toronto Rock and Roll Revival Festival and confided the same in Allen Klein, who had persuaded him to keep it quiet for the time being.

Above right and left, inset and opposite: John's commitment to the anti-war protest had hardened during the year and in November he returned his MBE to the Queen with a letter stating his reasons for doing so. As much an act of protest against US involvement in Vietnam, he also cited the UK's part in the Biafran War. As an afterthought, he added a third reason – "Cold Turkey" slipping down the charts. The press seized on the story and when interviewed on the radio, he explained that he had felt under pressure to accept the honour in 1965; the reference to his single was a joke as he didn't want the Queen thinking the letter was from "some boring colonel".

Bottom right: Yoko at home in the kitchen at Tittenhurst Park, a large Georgian mansion in Ascot, Berkshire. In December the BBC filmed her and John over five days at home and the 35-minute documentary received its first airing on BBC 1 on 15 December. John had plans to build a home recording studio at Tittenhurst and live a private, quiet life with Yoko.

We are anti-killing

Opposite and below centre and bottom: In a chance meeting with James Hanratty's parents at the end of 1969, John and Yoko took up the convicted murderer's cause. Hanratty had been hanged for the murder of a scientist in 1962 but irregularities in the case had led several prominent public figures to question the validity of the investigation and the eventual verdict.

In an interview in Canada the following week, Lennon maintained that he and Yoko were not "going down on any side whether the guy is innocent or not; we're anti-killing", a reference to their support for the abolition of the death penalty in Britain.

Top right: James Hanratty's mother sits beside a white bag in which John and Yoko make a silent protest against the execution of her son.

Below left and right: Arriving at the premiere for Ringo's film *The Magic Christian*, John and Yoko carry a placard reading "Britain Murdered Hanratty".

"One has to completely humiliate oneself to be what The Beatles were, and that's what I resent. I didn't know, I didn't foresee. It happened bit by bit, gradually, until this complete craziness is surrounding you, and you're doing exactly what you don't want to do with people you can't stand – the people you hated when you were ten.

"I want a divorce, just like the divorce I had from Cyn".

—John

The Plastic Ono Band

This page and opposite: The Plastic Ono Band was a conceptual idea of a band without members – "some pieces of plastic and a tape recorder" as John put it. In the middle of September the band's first show took place at the Toronto Rock and Roll Revival Festival. John had left it to the last minute to pull together a group of musicians but had managed to persuade Eric Clapton, Klaus Voorman and Alan White to join him and Yoko on stage; they performed six songs including the first live performance of "Give Peace A Chance". The band allowed John a greater degree of artistic freedom than he could have hoped for with The Beatles; no one quite knew what to expect from the new group.

"Peace for Christmas"

This page and opposite: The Plastic Ono Band played their second concert, entitled "Peace for Christmas", at the Lyceum Ballroom, London, in aid of the children's organization, UNICEF. The line-up included those from the Toronto gig as well as Keith Moon and George Harrison. The concert gave John and Yoko another opportunity to publicize their political and peace campaigns and to launch their "War is Over" poster campaign.

> The first time John performed in public without any of the other Beatles was a watershed moment. He found it exhilarating, convinced all the more that his allegiance lay exclusively with the new band.

John in Canada

The day after the UNICEF gig, John and Yoko flew to Toronto for a week-long round of press conferences and interviews. This included a meeting with the Canadian Prime Minister, Pierre Trudeau. Emerging from a 50-minute session with him, John remarked, "If all politicians were like Mr Trudeau there would be world peace".

Cold Turkey

The Plastic Ono band's second single was "Cold Turkey", a painfully honest account of John's attempts to withdraw from heroin, and a song which The Beatles did not feel comfortable with issuing. The 12th of December heralded the release of the band's first LP, a recording of their debut performance entitled *Live Peace In Toronto*.

JOHN LENNON TIMELINE

1969

3 Jan Thirty thousand copies of *Two Virgins* are confiscated in New Jersey on the grounds that the sleeve photography is pornographic.

18 Jan Apple's financial difficulties are revealed by John in an interview with *Disc and Music Echo*'s Ray Coleman.

30 Jan The Beatles perform together for the last time on the roof of the Apple building, London. The event is filmed as part of the *Let It Be* project.

2 Feb Yoko Ono is divorced from her husband Anthony Cox.

3 Feb Allen Klein is brought in to deal with The Beatles' finances, despite opposition from Paul.

2 Mar John and Yoko make an appearance at an avant-garde jazz performance in Cambridge.

20 Mar John and Yoko are married at the British Consulate in Gibraltar. They spend just over an hour there before flying back to Paris.

24 Mar John and Yoko have lunch with Salvador Dali in Paris.

25 Mar John and Yoko begin a week-long "bed-in" at the Amsterdam Hilton.

31 Mar John and Yoko fly to Vienna to launch their film *Rape*, which is premiered on television that night. They appear in a white bag for a brief press conference at the Hotel Sacher.

1 Apr John and Yoko appear on Thames Television's *Today* programme.

21 Apr John and Yoko's film and production company, Bag Productions, is formed.

22 Apr John changes his middle name to Ono at an official ceremony on the roof of the Apple building.

4 May John and Yoko buy their Berkshire mansion, Tittenhurst Park.

9 May John and Yoko's second album, *Unfinished Music No 2: Life With The Lions*, is released in the UK, on the newly formed Zapple label.

16 May John's 1968 drug conviction brings about the rejection of his application for a US visa.

26 May John and Yoko begin their second "bed-in" at the Queen Elizabeth Hotel, Montreal, Canada.

1 Jun "Give Peace a Chance" is recorded during the "bed-in" by the Plastic Ono Band, a makeshift group which includes John, Yoko and their friends, including guests such as Timothy Leary.

1 Jul John, Yoko, Yoko's daughter Kyoko and Julian are involved in a car crash in Scotland. John is hospitalized until 6 Jul.

3 Jul Perspex tubes, fitted with microphones, tape recorders and amplifiers stand in for the still-hospitalized John and Yoko at the launch of the Plastic Ono Band in London.

4 Jul John's first solo single, "Give Peace a Chance", is released, credited to the Plastic Ono Band.

22 Aug The last photograph of all The Beatles together is taken at John and Yoko's home, Tittenhurst Park.

1 Sept John, Yoko, George, Pattie, Ringo and Maureen (Ringo's wife) see Bob Dylan play at the Isle of Wight Festival.

10 Sept The New Cinema Club holds an evening of John and Yoko's films, at the ICA, where a couple, possibly John and Yoko, sit on stage throughout, contained within a white bag.

13 Sept John decides to quit The Beatles while on his way to a hastily arranged concert in Toronto with the Plastic Ono Band; his decision is not made public.

26 Sept "Abbey Road" is released.

12 Oct Yoko has a second miscarriage at King's College Hospital, London. John resumes his use of heroin, which he had been attempting to stop.

24 Oct The Plastic Ono Band release "Cold Turkey" as a UK single.

3/10 Nov Nash House, London, holds two nights of John and Yoko's films, under the title *Something Else*.

7 Nov John and Yoko release their *Wedding Album* in the UK in a luxurious package.

13 Nov John Lennon offers a tiny island, Dornish, rent-free to a group of hippies.

25 Nov John returns his MBE to Buckingham Palace, in protest against government policy over Nigeria, military action in Vietnam, and the poor chart performance of his latest single.

10 Dec John and Yoko meet the parents of James Hanratty, a convicted murderer, who was hanged in 1962. They plan to make a film proving his innocence.

11 Dec John carries a banner outside the premiere of Ringo's *The Magic Christian*, proclaiming, "Britain Murdered Hanratty".

12 Dec The Plastic Ono Band release the LP *Live Peace in Toronto* worldwide.

14 Dec John and Yoko protest silently, inside a white bag, at Speakers' Corner, Marble Arch, over the hanging of Hanratty. Later a petition is handed in to 10 Downing Street.

15 Dec John and Yoko appear with the Plastic Ono Band, featuring Yoko, Eric Clapton, Billy Preston and Keith Moon, at a UNICEF charity concert at the Lyceum Ballroom, London.

23 Dec John and Yoko have a private meeting with Canada's Prime Minister, Pierre Trudeau in Ottawa, Canada.

24 Dec John and Yoko briefly join a sit-in in Kent.

29 Dec John and Yoko fly to Denmark to holiday with Kyoko, her father Anthony Cox and his wife Melinda.

30 Dec John is featured in a three-part programme on ITV, *Man of The Decade*, which also includes John F. Kennedy and Mao Tse Tung.

CHAPTER EIGHT

EARLY SEVENTIES

Nothing's gonna change my world

In January 1970 when Paul, George and Ringo came together in the studio to record George's song "I, Me, Mine" for the album *Let It Be*, John was not there with them. He was with Yoko in Denmark, from where he announced that all the proceeds from his music would in future be used to promote peace. He had now almost totally turned his attention away from The Beatles and towards what he was doing with Yoko, particularly in the areas of conceptual and avant-garde art. Later in the month an exhibition of his lithographs, *Bag One*, opened at the London Arts Gallery, featuring a series of erotic pictures depicting them on their honeymoon. Almost immediately, the exhibition was raided and closed down by the police, and eight pictures were confiscated for being obscene. However, just over three months later the courts decided that the pictures were not indecent after all, and they were all returned. John and Yoko did not come back from Denmark until the end of January, when they appeared in London with their hair cropped short. They later gave their tresses to Michael X in return for a pair of Muhammad Ali's boxing shorts, which they planned to auction to raise money for their peace campaign.

The Plastic Ono Band was still releasing records – and even appeared on BBC television's *Top of the Pops*, performing a recently released single, "Instant Karma". In keeping with John's belief that music should be more immediate, "Instant Karma" had been both written and recorded within the space of just one day.

In March John revealed to the French magazine *L'Express* that he and the other Beatles had smoked cannabis in the toilets at Buckingham Palace, before they were presented with their MBEs in 1965. The same month he broadcast a message to a CND rally in London, during which he mentioned that Yoko was pregnant for the third time. Unfortunately, she lost the baby again.

The rifts within The Beatles were still not public knowledge, but in April, in a press release for his album, *McCartney*, Paul effectively said he was leaving the group. For years afterwards Paul was blamed for precipitating the break-up, when actually he had been the last to go. John was furious – he had been talked out of making public his decision to leave, and now Paul had beaten him to it. He bitterly resented Paul appearing to be the decision-maker, just as he had resented him trying to lead The Beatles after Brian Epstein's death.

In his personal life, despite his fulfilling and exciting partnership with Yoko, John found he was still having problems that he felt dated back to his troubled childhood. During this period he was introduced to the work of Dr Janov, who proposed a therapy called "primal scream" to cure neurosis. He and Yoko went through a course of this therapy with Janov himself, which certainly seemed to help John come to terms with a great many of his hang-ups, and led to him writing soul-baring songs such as "Mother" and "God". The therapy also precipitated a serious argument with his father, who had come to see John at Tittenhurst Park with his wife, about the events of his childhood. It was the last time John saw

Opposite: John and Yoko return from Denmark in late January 1970 sporting cropped haircuts. In the same month, the final song on the *Let It Be* album was recorded without John.

Fred, although he did speak to his father again on the phone before Fred died in 1976 – by which time John was living permanently in America.

Several of John's continuing worries were to do with the business affairs of The Beatles. Their contractual arrangements were in a mess, and Allen Klein discovered that, despite what they had been led to believe, *Yellow Submarine* did not constitute the third in their three-film contract with United Artists. Fortunately there was enough material from *Get Back*, their abortive documentary, to make a full-length feature film instead. The revised project, now called *Let It Be*, was sold to UA and was premiered in New York in May 1970 – none of The Beatles attended.

Although The Beatles as a group were officially no more, with each member set on a solo career, the four of them were still legally tied together until 1975 by The Beatles & Co., the company they had formed three years earlier. Under the terms of their agreement, all of the income any of them made, even from their solo albums, was to be split four ways. At the end of December 1970, Paul decided he had had enough of abortive discussions with the others and he filed a lawsuit in London, seeking dissolution of The Beatles & Co. and the appointment of a receiver to sort out the group's affairs. The High Court case was heard in London during February and March 1971 and Paul, supported by his wife, Linda, was the only Beatle to attend. It soon became apparent that Klein's company had taken at least $500,000 more than they were entitled to, and the judge finally ruled in favour of Paul.

Meanwhile, John and Yoko had become deeply involved in film making, and in creating avant-garde art films. After *Rape* they made *Erection* – although its title may have led the audience to expect something different, this actually showed the progress of a hotel being erected in London over a nine-month period. Two of their films, *Apotheosis (Balloon)* and *Fly*, were premiered at the Cannes Film Festival in May 1971. *Apotheosis (Balloon)* simply showed a balloon taking off from a field, while the soundtrack of everyday noises fades away to silence.

Although Yoko's divorce from Anthony Cox had been reasonably amicable, in 1971 he vanished with Kyoko. John and Yoko believed that he had taken her to New York, so in June they flew to America to look for her. They later returned to England for a few months, during which time they attended the signing for the official release of *Grapefruit*, Yoko's book that previously had only been available in a limited edition. They also made their last public appearance in the UK, when they were both interviewed on the *Parkinson* show on network television. In September they returned to New York for a short

visit, which turned into a permanent stay. Part of the reason was that Yoko soon started legal proceedings to win custody of Kyoko, but they also decided they felt more comfortable in New York. Yoko had spent a great deal of time there when she was younger, and she showed John round and introduced him to her favourite haunts. The press in Britain had ridiculed them and their beliefs, and had made fun of Yoko as an artist, but in America they seemed less critical and more open to new ideas.

Towards the end of 1971, John released *Imagine*, one of his most critically acclaimed solo albums, which topped the charts in both Britain and America. The songs were gentler – more commercial and less avant-garde – than those he had released previously. However, he also included a bitter attack on Paul in a song called "How Do You Sleep?" in answer to several songs on Paul's LP, *Ram*, which had included some rather pointed lyrics against John and Yoko. Now that it was out in the open, the quarrel continued in public. In an interview with *Melody Maker* in November 1971, Paul complained that he just wanted to sort out their business problems between the four of them, but that John was refusing to meet. John's letter of reply was published two weeks later. It was a bitter attack on Paul, pointing out that he had been the one to instigate the lawsuit and that they couldn't just sort out the business between themselves as there were ongoing problems with the taxman to resolve. It was to be four years before the two of them met again, in New York, and even then the animosity between them was still not fully resolved.

Meanwhile, John was settling into his new life in New York. At the end of October he was a guest artist at Yoko's exhibition, *This Is Not Here*, and later that month, he and Yoko invited the children of the Harlem Community Choir to join them to record "Happy Christmas (War Is Over)". It was released as a single in the US at the beginning of December, and quickly became a classic Christmas song – although it was nearly a year later before it was available in the UK.

They also continued to work for peace and against injustice – in December they appeared at a benefit rally for writer John Sinclair, who had been imprisoned in 1969 for ten years, for possession of a very small amount of marijuana. He was released on bail just over two days later. However, both John and Yoko's US visas were about to expire – and by now the US authorities had begun to realize that John would continue speaking out on controversial issues and that his views were listened to and respected by a wide range of people.

Above: John outside the Apple offices holding a copy of "Power to the People". Recorded with the Plastic Ono Band, it was a politically charged single reflecting his deepening involvement in political issues.

> "I'd like to live to a ripe old age, with Yoko only, you know. And I'm not afraid of dying. I don't know how it'd feel at the moment. But I'm prepared for death because I don't believe in it. I think it's just getting out of one car and getting into another." —John

War is Over

Above and right inset: John and Yoko launch their War is Over campaign, with posters and billboards displayed in cities around the world. John used the slogan in 1971 as the basis of his hit Christmas single, 'Happy Xmas (War is Over)'

Right: At the beginning of 1970, John and Yoko spent time in Denmark where Yoko's daughter, Kyoko, was staying with her father, Tony Cox. The trip meant John missed The Beatles' last recording session as a group.

Opposite: John's *Bag One* exhibition opens at the London Arts Gallery in New Bond Street in mid-January 1970. It consisted of a set of lithographs drawn by him in 1969 chronicling his wedding and honeymoon, including one of the world-peace "bed-ins". Some of the images were undoubtedly erotic and following a tip-off, the police raided the gallery the next day. Eight artworks were removed on the grounds of obscenity but in fact, John was not prosecuted under the Obscene Publications Act. Instead, the offence was cited as distributing indecent material in a public thoroughfare. The case was thrown out three weeks into the trial and the lithographs were returned.

Opposite bottom left: In July 1970 Cynthia Lennon marries Italian hotelier Roberto Bassini at Kensington Register Office; Julian was a page boy.

Instant Karma

Above: John and The Plastic Ono Band performing "Instant Karma!" on *Top of the Pops* in February 1970. Yoko sits beside him crocheting and wearing a blindfold; both are sporting armbands with the words "People for Peace". The Beatles had appeared on the show five times but John was the first member to appear solo; his vocals were live. His third single with the Plastic Ono Band, "Instant Karma!" was written and recorded on the same day and released ten days later. At the press launch, John quipped, "...wrote it for breakfast, recorded it for lunch and we're putting it out for dinner." The band line-up on this occasion was John, Klaus Voorman, Mal Evans, Alan White and Yoko.

During the spring, John and Yoko underwent Primal Therapy, a trauma-based psychotherapy with the US psychotherapist Arthur Janov. After the experience, John commented, "I no longer have any need for drugs, the Maharishi or The Beatles. I am myself and I know why".

Opposite top left: While staying in Aalborg, Denmark, at Tony Cox's farmhouse John and Yoko cut their hair – reportedly a do-it-yourself job. Reasons for the dramatic change in image varied from keeping the publicity alive for the peace campaign to the polar opposite of John wanting to be able to travel incognito. If the latter, it proved to be a failure – the press soon got wind of the news and pictures of their shorn heads were made public.

Right: Throughout the early 1970s John and Yoko were involved in a custody dispute with Tony Cox. Here John is dressed formally to attend a custody hearing in a Houston Court House.

This page: In February the pair met Michael X, the civil rights activist and leader of the Black Power organization, at its headquarters in Holloway, London. They exchanged a bag of their shorn hair for a pair of Muhammad Ali's bloodstained shorts. It was planned that both items be auctioned for peace causes later in the year.

> "I could see us not working together for a period but we'd always get together for one reason or another. I mean you need other people for ideas as well but you know… we all get along fine." —**John**

Let It Be

Throughout the first few months of 1970, all four of The Beatles were working on solo projects and were rarely seen together, although an official announcement of their split had not yet been made.

The strained relations between John and Paul in particular had calmed to a certain extent and much of their communication was through letters rather than face-to-face. The animosity flared up again when a clash over release dates for *Let It Be* and Paul's debut album *McCartney* came up. Releasing both close together would damage sales and John decided The Beatles' album should have precedence, pushing back Paul's solo release until June.

Delivering the news to him with a letter from John and George, Ringo took the brunt of Paul's rage. In the event, *McCartney* was released on its original planned date and *Let It Be* three weeks later. In the press release for his debut album, Paul made it clear that The Beatles had split up.

JOHN LENNON TIMELINE

1970-71

3/4 Jan Paul, George and Ringo record together for *Let It Be*, their last recording session in John's lifetime. John is absent.

5 Jan John makes the announcement that all proceeds from his music will in future be used to promote peace.

15 Jan John's exhibition of lithographs, *Bag One*, opens in London.

16 Jan *Bag One* is closed as police confiscate eight lithographs depicting John and Yoko, for reasons of obscenity.

20 Jan John and Yoko have their hair cropped in Denmark.

22 Jan John's lithographs go on show in the US at Detroit's London Arts Gallery.

27 Jan John writes and records "Instant Karma".

4 Feb John and Yoko swap their recently shorn hair for a pair of Muhammad Ali's boxing shorts with Michael X, leader of Black Power. They intend to auction them to raise money for peace causes.

6 Feb John and Yoko release "Instant Karma"/ "Who Has Seen The Wind?" in the UK.

12 Feb The Plastic Ono Band perform "Instant Karma" on the BBC's *Top of the Pops*.

22 Mar John reveals in an interview with *L'Express*, a French magazine, that The Beatles smoked cannabis in the toilets at Buckingham Palace in 1965.

29 Mar A message is broadcast at a CND rally in London, in which John reveals Yoko is pregnant for a third time.

10 Apr Paul announces his resignation from The Beatles.

23 Apr John and Yoko go to LA for a course of primal scream therapy.

27 Apr John's lithographs are returned, after a court decides they are not indecent.

8 Dec John is interviewed by *Rolling Stone*. The interview is published in two parts in early 1971, and later, as "Lennon Remembers".

11 Dec The LP *John Lennon / The Plastic Ono Band* is released worldwide.

31 Dec Paul begins proceedings to end the partnership of The Beatles.

1971

19 Feb The hearing to dissolve The Beatles & Co. Partnership commences in the London High Court.

12 Mar John and Yoko release "Power To The People"/ "Open Your Box" as a single in the UK.

12 Mar The High Court judge rules in Paul's favour.

15 May Two of John and Yoko's films, *Apotheosis (Balloon)* and *Fly*, premiere at the Cannes Film Festival.

31 May John is granted a US visa for nine months.

1 Jun John and Yoko fly to New York to try to locate Kyoko, and to gain custody of her.

6 Jun John meets Frank Zappa, later appearing live with Yoko, and Zappa's band The Mothers of Invention at New York's Fillmore East.

Jul John finishes the album *Imagine*.

15 Jul John and Yoko attend a signing, promoting the re-publication of Yoko's *Grapefruit*.

17 Jul John and Yoko make their last UK public appearance, interviewed on *Parkinson*.

11 Aug John and Yoko are amongst demonstrators in London, opposing internment in Northern Ireland, and the *Oz* magazine editors who are being tried for obscenity.

3 Sept John and Yoko fly to New York. The "visit" becomes a permanent stay.

9 Sept John appears on *The Dick Cavett Show*, explaining the disbanding of The Beatles.

8 Oct The LP *Imagine* sees its UK release.

9-27 Oct John is a guest artist at Yoko's *This Is Not Here* exhibition in New York.

6 Nov John and Yoko appear at a benefit in New York after demonstrations over the Attica Prison riots.

1 Dec "Happy Christmas (War Is Over)" is issued as a single in the US (24 November 1972 in the UK).

4 Dec John attacks Paul in the *Melody Maker*'s letters page.

11 Dec John and Yoko appear at a rally for writer John Sinclair who was imprisoned in 1969 for ten years on charges of marijuana possession. He is released on bail just over two days later.

"We'll probably carry on writing music forever, you know, whatever else we're doing. 'Cos you just can't stop, you find yourself doing it whether you want to or not." —**John**

Top and inset: John and Yoko promote their single "Power to the People" which was released in March 1971. Yoko's "Open Your Box" was on the B-side in the UK but in the US the song was replaced by "Touch Me", another Yoko Ono song with less controversial lyrics.

John's final appearance in the UK

Right: Early in the summer of 1971, John and Yoko flew to New York to find Yoko's daughter Kyoko, who had been taken there by her father Tony Cox. Yoko had legal custody of Kyoko but Cox disappeared with their daughter and joined a religious cult. She and Yoko did not meet again until 1994. Returning from the States, John and Yoko attended a signing event for the release of her book *Grapefruit* – a conceptual piece, it contained over 150 "instruction works" on music, painting and poetry. The pair also made their last public appearance in the UK on the BBC show *Parkinson*.

Below: John and Yoko wait for their flight to Nice and the Cannes Film Festival in May 1971. Their short films *Apotheosis* and *Fly* were screened but John and Yoko were disappointed with the public reaction. *Apotheosis* showed the journey of a balloon ascending into the clouds. *Fly* was shot in close-up and followed a fly as it walked over the naked body of a woman.

Imagine released and tops the charts

Opposite: On 3 September 1971 John and Yoko leave for the US for what was planned as a short visit, moving into an apartment in Greenwich Village after a few days. While there, John's second solo album, *Imagine,* was released. Much of the work on the record was done at the end of May in the studio John had set up at Tittenhurst Park but the album was completed in early July 1971 at Record Plant East studio in New York. *Imagine* was a critical success, it also pleased the fans and topped the charts both sides of the Atlantic.

The title track of *Imagine*, co-written by John and Yoko (although she did not receive recognition for this until 2017), turned out to be the best-selling single of Lennon's career. Its political message of a world without borders or religious divisions was commercially appealing because of its simple, haunting melody. John himself described its anti-religious, anti-nationalistic message as being "sugar-coated... with a little honey".

Left and above: The trip to New York in September 1971 proved to be a permanent stay and the release of *Imagine* was followed by Yoko's retrospective art exhibition *This Is Not He*re. John quickly settled in the US, becoming involved in the politics of the radical left and participating in demonstrations and rallies. It wasn't long before this drew increased attention from the US authorities and his fight to resist deportation as an undesirable and remain in the States began.

Although he could not have known it at the time, when John left London on 3 September 1971, he would never return to Britain.

"How Do You Sleep?" was an attack on Paul but in general, the songs on *Imagine* were gentler and a move away from the avant-garde creations for the Plastic Ono Band.

CHAPTER NINE

LIFE IN AMERICA

Nobody told me there'd be days like these

Although 1972 began well, with John and Yoko demonstrating outside the BOAC building to support a boycott of UK exports as a protest against British policy in Northern Ireland, and hosting *The Mike Douglas Show* – on which John performed with Chuck Berry, one of his teenage idols – it quickly deteriorated. At the end of February both John and Yoko's US visas expired, although they were both granted routine temporary fifteen-day extensions to allow them to make fresh applications. Soon afterwards, Yoko was awarded custody of Kyoko, but before the child could be handed over her father took her into hiding. A few days later, both John and Yoko's temporary visa extensions were suddenly cancelled, and they were served with deportation orders, citing John's 1968 drugs conviction. Yoko immediately appealed, saying that they would lose custody of her daughter if they left America – even though Kyoko still had not been found. It was quickly apparent that John's drug conviction had little to do with what was happening – John and Yoko's friends in New York included a whole crowd of left-wing radicals and political activists, and the American government had taken note. Even the mayor of New York, John Lindsay, wrote to the immigration board to say that the real reason the couple were being deported was because they spoke out on issues of the day. Not long afterwards, during an appearance on *The Dick Cavett Show*, John claimed his privacy was being invaded by government agents. It was the beginning of his long battle against deportation – although Yoko was granted permanent residency in March 1973, at the same time John was ordered to leave the US within sixty days.

Despite the 1971 High Court ruling, The Beatles' joint business affairs took a long while to untangle. Allen Klein and ABKCO did not reach the end of their term as business managers of Apple and the other Beatles companies until the end of March 1973, and The Beatles & Co. partnership was not formally dissolved until January 1975. The strain of all this, and of fighting the deportation order, had its effect on John and Yoko's marriage. John could be volatile and difficult to live with at the best of times; when he was under stress he retreated into himself and also tended to drink too much. Unfortunately, he couldn't handle alcohol – he often became abusive and sometimes violent. Towards the end of 1973 Yoko decided that time apart would do them both good and John went to Los Angeles with their secretary, May Pang. What was supposed to be a temporary separation turned into a fifteen-month "lost weekend", as John settled into a house with Keith Moon and Ringo and the three of them over-indulged in both drink and drugs. May was good company and she looked after John well, but he still loved Yoko and missed her the entire time. However, Yoko would not allow him to return until she felt he had worked through some of his fantasies and hang-ups. John himself later referred to this period as a "grow-up time".

Opposite: John and Yoko attend the Grammy Awards ceremony in 1975, where John presents the award for "Record of the Year". It was the couple's first public appearance together since their reconciliation after John's "Lost Weekend".

Meanwhile, he continued his fight against deportation, suing the US government over alleged illegal wiretapping and FBI surveillance, claiming in court that attempts to deport him were based on his involvement in anti-war demonstrations and not on his drug conviction, and requesting the right to question officials about an alleged police vendetta. He was ordered to leave the US again, but again he appealed. By now he was supported by many influential people in the US, and the groundswell of public opinion was firmly behind him. Despite everything else that was going on during this period, he did not neglect his music – he managed to produce two good albums, *Walls and Bridges*, and *Rock 'n' Roll*.

After Klein was accused of irregularities in his accounting, following one of George's concerts for charity, relations between all four Beatles were much improved. The others had to admit that Paul's fears about him had been justified and in November 1973 John, George and Ringo sued Klein for misrepresentation in the High Court. Paul and John began to communicate again, and Paul even visited John while he was in Los Angeles and the two played together.

In November 1974 John kept a promise to perform at Elton John's Thanksgiving Concert in New York, and met up with Yoko again backstage. Within a couple of months he had returned to live with her in New York – and they soon announced that she was expecting a baby. John's deportation was delayed because of the pregnancy and the following month the order was finally reversed by the New York State Senate.

After their son, Sean, was born on John's thirty-fifth birthday, 9 October 1975, John announced he was taking five years off to focus on bringing up his child, while Yoko carried on working. They settled in New York permanently, and John was granted his Green Card in July 1976. This meant he could safely leave the US without fear of being refused permission to return; in June 1977, he, Yoko and Sean were able to go to Japan for five months to visit Yoko's family.

At the beginning of 1980, John and Yoko bought a seafront mansion in Florida, where they celebrated their eleventh wedding anniversary. Later that year, John went on holiday alone to Cape Town, South Africa, and soon afterwards he began to compose again.

Having almost completed the promised five years looking after Sean, John also began to record again and soon brought out a new album, *Double Fantasy*, just in

time for his son's fifth birthday in October. The reviews were good and in public John seemed happy and full of enthusiasm. He began to move back into the public eye, doing a huge, three-week interview, along with Yoko, for *Playboy*, and shorter interviews for *Newsweek* and *Rolling Stone*, as well as radio interviews for BBC's Radio 1 with Andy Peebles and RKO radio.

Early on 8 December, as John came out of the Dakota Building where he and Yoko lived in New York, he was stopped by 'a fan' and signed a copy of *Double Fantasy* for him. This person then waited outside the building all day, until John returned home from the studio late that night. As John headed towards his home, five shots were fired at point-blank range. Although he was rushed to hospital, he was pronounced dead on arrival.

The sense of grief and outrage at his death was overwhelming all around the world, but was even more hysterical in America. In Britain there had been little news of him over the previous few years, but in the US he had captured the hearts of those opposed to the war in Vietnam and had been known as an outspoken opponent of any kind of injustice. Many felt they had lost an inspirational leader. On 14 December Yoko called for ten minutes of silence to be observed at 7.00 pm GMT around the world in his memory, and throughout December the airwaves were full of the sound of "Imagine", one of his best-loved songs.

In memory of John, a large area of New York's Central Park was renamed Strawberry Fields. At the site-opening ceremony in March 1984, attended by Yoko, Sean and Julian, Yoko revealed that it was where she and John had gone on their last walk together. She appealed for every country to send something for the planned garden, as a tribute to John. Many responded, and when the finished garden was opened in October 1985 it contained plants from all round the world.

One unexpected result of John's death was that the other three Beatles started to collaborate again. Right back in the 1970s the four of them had planned to produce a documentary that would tell their story in their own words, tentatively titled *The Long And Winding Road*. The project had suffered the same fate as many others during their break-up – the four of them could never agree on how things should be done. Now the three remaining Beatles came together to produce a television documentary and three double albums, all entitled *The Beatles Anthology*. Paul, George and Ringo were interviewed for the project and John was included in the form of old interviews, mainly from his solo days. Yoko had sent them some tapes of John, including several unfinished songs, sparking off the idea that the three of them should finish them off. It was not so dissimilar to how they had worked in the old days, and towards the end of 1995 the first single, "Free as a Bird", was released along with the television documentary. Newspapers ran whole pages devoted to the "Fab Four", and magazines brought out special issues – even after twenty-five years The Beatles were big news.

In May 2002, twenty-two years after John's death, the readers of The *Guardian* newspaper took part in a Jubilee poll to establish the person who had done more to shape Britain during the fifty years of Queen Elizabeth II's reign than the Queen herself. The final list included politicians, entertainers and scientists; The Beatles came joint sixth, but the man who brought them together came in at number one. John Lennon may be gone, but in the hearts and minds of many all round the world he is certainly not forgotten.

Above: Five-year-old Paula Carney is held aloft in the crowds that gathered in Liverpool in March 1981 to remember John. A Festival of Peace at Liverpool Cathedral attracted thousands, many of whom spilled into the streets of the city when the cathedral was full.

JOHN LENNON TIMELINE: 1972 – 1980

1972

5 Feb John and Yoko participate in protests supporting a boycott of British exports in response to the British policy in Northern Ireland.

14—18 Feb John and Yoko host *The Mike Douglas Show*. John performs with Chuck Berry, a teenage idol of his.

29 Feb John and Yoko's US visas expire.

3 Mar Yoko is awarded custody of Kyoko, but Kyoko's father takes her into hiding.

6 Mar John and Yoko's temporary visa extensions are cancelled.

16 Mar John is served with a deportation order which cites his 1968 drug conviction.

22 Apr John and Yoko protest against US action in Vietnam at the National Peace Rally in New York.

29 Apr An announcement is made of a written appeal from the mayor of New York City, John Lindsay, which calls for the deportation orders against John and Yoko to be dropped.

11 May John appears on *The Dick Cavett Show* claiming that his privacy is being invaded by government agents.

12 Jun John and Yoko release their double LP, *Sometime In New York City* in the US (15 September in the UK).

30 Aug John and Yoko stage two charity concerts in New York at Madison Square Garden.

23 Dec John and Yoko's film *Imagine* premieres on US television.

1973

23 Mar John is ordered to leave the US within sixty days, while Yoko is granted permanent residency. John formally appeals the following day.

Oct John embarks upon his "lost weekend", separating from Yoko and flying to LA with their secretary, May Pang.

24 Oct John sues the US government over alleged FBI surveillance.

Oct—Dec John records a rock and roll album produced by Phil Spector.

2 Nov John, George and Ringo sue Allen Klein for misrepresentation in the High Court. Klein counter-sues.

2 Nov US release of LP *Mind Games* and "Mind Games"/ "Meat City" single (16 November in the UK).

1974

13 Mar John is thrown out of the Troubadour nightclub for disrupting a Smothers Brothers concert.

27 Mar A complaint against John, made by a waitress from the Troubadour is dismissed by the LA district attorney.

17 Jul John is again given sixty days to leave the US.

31 Aug John claims that attempts at his deportation centre around his involvement in anti-war demonstrations, rather than his drug conviction.

23 Sept John releases "Whatever Gets You Through The Night"/ "Beef Jerky" as a single in the US (4 Oct in the UK).

26 Sept John releases his *Walls And Bridges* LP in the US (4 Oct in the UK).

28 Oct Allen Klein loses his court case against John, Ringo and George.

16 Nov John has his first US solo No.1 with "Whatever Gets You Through The Night". Elton John plays keyboards on the track.

28 Nov John sings three songs with Elton John at Madison Square Garden.

16 Dec John issues "#9 Dream"/ "What You Got" as a US single (31 Jan 1975 in the UK).

27 Dec John, Julian and May Pang holiday in Disneyland.

1975

Jan John records with David Bowie.

Jan John returns to Yoko in New York.

9 Jan The Beatles & Co. is formally dissolved in the London High Court.

17 Feb John's LP *Rock 'n' Roll* is released in the US (21 Feb in the UK).

6 Mar John issues a statement that his separation from Yoko is over.

10 Mar The single "Stand By Me"/ "Move Over Mrs L", is released in the US (18 Apr in the UK).

18 Apr John gives his last performance before an audience, on *A Salute To Lew Grade*, television special.

23 Sept John's deportation is delayed due to Yoko's pregnancy.

7 Oct The deportation order, which John has been fighting for some years, is reversed by the New York State Senate.

9 Oct Sean Taro Ono Lennon is born to John and Yoko on John's thirty-fifth birthday.

24 Oct "Working Class Hero" is released in the UK only.

1976

5 Jan The Beatles' former tour manager, Mal Evans, is shot dead by police in LA.

26 Jan The Beatles' recording contract with EMI expires; Paul stays with EMI, George and Ringo move to other labels, and John does not sign with anyone.

1 Apr John's father, Fred, dies in hospital in Brighton, England.

27 Jul John finally receives his Green Card.

Oct John decides to retire from music in order to focus on bringing up Sean.

1977

10 Jan All outstanding litigation is settled with Allen Klein.

20 Jan John and Yoko attend the inauguration of Jimmy Carter as President in Washington DC.

4 Apr The Beatles attempt to stop the release of an LP recorded in Hamburg in 1962, but fail.

Jun John, Yoko and Sean go to Japan for five months.

1978

4 Feb John and Yoko buy land in Delaware County, and it is revealed they are buying several other apartments in the Dakota building where they are residents.

16 Jun John attempts to prevent the *News of The World* from publishing extracts from his first wife's, Cynthia's, book, *A Twist Of Lennon*, but is unsuccessful.

1979

27 May John and Yoko place adverts in newspapers in London, Tokyo and New York, entitled "A Love Letter From John And Yoko, To People Who Ask Us What, When And Why".

15 Oct $1000 is donated by John and Yoko to help to provide bullet-proof vests for the New York police.

31 Dec Various ventures which were established in the late 1960s are dissolved, including John and Yoko's film and production company, Bag Productions.

1980

28 Jan John and Yoko buy a seafront mansion in Florida.

20 Mar John and Yoko celebrate their eleventh wedding anniversary in Florida. Yoko gives John a vintage Rolls-Royce.

23 May John travels alone to Cape Town, South Africa.

Jul John begins to compose again, in Bermuda.

4 Aug John and Yoko begin studio work for a new album at the Hit Factory studio, Manhattan.

9 Sept John and Yoko begin a huge interview for *Playboy*, lasting almost three weeks.

22 Sept Yoko signs a recording contract for herself and John with the newly formed independent label, Geffen Records.

29 Sept *Newsweek* publishes the first interview with John and Yoko to appear in several years.

9 Oct Yoko has a message sky-written for John's fortieth birthday and Sean's fifth.

27 Oct John releases the single "(Just Like) Starting Over"/ "Kiss Kiss Kiss" in the US (24 Oct in the UK).

17 Nov John and Yoko release the album *Double Fantasy*.

5 Dec John records an interview with *Rolling Stone* magazine.

6 Dec John and Yoko record an interview together for BBC's Radio 1, with Andy Peebles.

8 Dec John and Yoko record an interview with RKO Radio.

8 Dec (9 Dec in the UK) John is shot and killed outside the Dakota apartment building in New York.

10 Dec John is cremated at Hartsdale Crematorium, New York State.

14 Dec Ten minutes' silence is observed around the world, at 7pm GMT, in memory of John.

14 Dec Extracts from the RKO interview are broadcast in the US.

20 Dec "(Just Like) Starting Over" goes to No. 1 in the UK, having previously slipped down the charts from 8th to 21st position.

27 Dec "(Just Like) Starting Over" reaches the No.1 spot in the US, where it is to remain for five weeks. *Double Fantasy* tops the album chart.

John's "Lost Weekend"

Opposite and right: By the autumn of 1973, the custody battle for Kyoko and the fight against deportation had taken its toll on the Lennon—Ono marriage. By mutual consent, they decided to have some time apart and Lennon left New York for California, accompanied by their secretary, May Pang.

Without Yoko's stabilizing influence, John indulged in drinking and partying and began an affair with May Pang. His "lost weekend", as he called it, lasted 15 months before he returned to New York in the summer of 1974. He wrote and recorded *Walls and Bridges* and released the chart-topping single "Whatever Gets You Through the Night", featuring backing vocals from Elton John.

Returning the favour, John joined Elton on stage at his Thanksgiving Concert in Madison Square Garden in November – Lennon's last concert appearance. Yoko was in the audience that night and they met backstage. In the New Year, John returned to their apartment in the Dakota Building on Central Park.

Below: In response to the US immigration authorities' order for John to leave the US within 60 days, he and Yoko hold a press conference to announce their appeal against the decision and the birth of "Nutopia", a conceptual country with no boundaries or land or passports – only people. They declare themselves citizens of the country.

> "We've basically decided, without a great decision, to be with our baby as much as we can, until we feel we can take the time off to indulge ourselves creating things outside the family. Maybe when he's three, four, or five, then we'll think about creating something else other than the child. —**John**

> "In London, I couldn't walk around the block. I would be walking around tense, like waiting for somebody to say something or jump on me, and it took me two years to unwind. I can go right out of this door now and go in a restaurant or to the movies – you want to know how great that is?"—**John**

John and Sean

Top: John with Sean in 1977 in New York. Sean Tara Ono Lennon was born on John's birthday in 1975 in New York. It marked the start of a five-year retirement from the public eye for John to allow him to focus on the upbringing of his son, and to allow Yoko to pursue her own career. Shortly after the birth, John is quoted as saying, "I feel higher than the Empire State Building!" and in 1980, he called Sean his "biggest pride".

Right: John and Yoko in New York. Having returned to New York, John rescued his *Rock 'n' Roll* album tapes from Phil Spector – to whom he had entrusted the project during the "lost weekend" period. In February 1975 he released *Rock 'n' Roll*, his sixth and final studio album before he retired to look after his son, Sean. The album consisted of 1950s and '60s song covers recorded while he and Yoko were separated.

Lennon and McCartney were by now on good terms and Paul would visit John at the Dakota Building when he was in town. In April 1976, the pair, together

with Yoko and Linda, were watching *Saturday Live* when the producer made an on-air, tongue-in-cheek offer for The Beatles to re-unite on the show. For a moment John and Paul considered the possibility of going down to the TV studio that night as a joke but the moment passed. Although they remained in touch, the following day was the last time the song-writing duo met face-to-face.

Double Fantasy

John continued to write music during his period as a full-time carer for Sean. He spent some time over the summer of 1980 in Bermuda, where he began writing in earnest again, committing several songs to tape. Upon his return to New York, he went into the studio with Yoko to begin work on *Double Fantasy* and by September, most of the album was complete.

John's comeback was gathering momentum. The first single from the album, "(Just Like) Starting Over", was released at the end of October and the LP in mid-November. John had also met up with George Harrison and Ringo on separate occasions in the previous months.

Interviews were given to various publications and it was announced that he would embark on a tour of the US and Europe. On 6 December John explained to his aunt Mimi that he hoped to return to Britain soon. He also gave an interview to BBC Radio's Andy Peebles that day.

> 66
>
> "I've always considered my work one piece and I consider that my work won't be finished until I am dead and buried and I hope that's a long, long time." —**John**

Daily Mail

MONEY MAIL TODAY

Mail Picture Exclusive–The autograph that led to murder

LENNON AND HIS KILLER

Yoko: pray for John

It was quite usual for fans to stand vigil outside the Dakota Building for a glimpse of their favourite Beatle and perhaps be lucky enough to gain an autograph (below inset).

On the afternoon of 8 December 1980, as he and Yoko left their apartment building for the Record Plant studio, one such fan approached him to ask for his signature on the *Double Fantasy* album; John duly obliged. Returning several hours later, the same "fan" – stepped out of the shadows where he had been waiting and shot Lennon five times at close range. Despite a rapid response from the emergency services, John was declared dead on arrival at Roosevelt Hospital.

Within hours, the police had held a press conference to confirm John's death and as the news spread, crowds began gathering outside the Dakota Building. Tributes filled the newspapers and across radio and TV. Ringo and his girlfriend, Barbara Bach, travelled to New York to be with Yoko and Sean, and Julian Lennon flew in. The following day, Yoko issued a statement telling the world that there would not be a funeral and asking people to pray for John; he was cremated on 10 December.

John's murderer was sent to Attica Correctional Facility, a maximum-security prison in New York State. He has been denied parole ten times.

Candlelit vigils for John

Thousands of fans gathered in St George's Square, Liverpool, for a memorial service and a candlelit vigil on 14 December. Similar vigils were held in New York and other cities in the US; a ten-minute silence was observed in the evening.

Double Fantasy, released three weeks earlier, to less than critical acclaim, became an immediate hit after Lennon's death, reaching No. 1 in the US where it remained for 11 weeks. The single "(Just Like) Starting Over" was also a commercial success. Throughout the following year, John's anthemic "Imagine" and "Give Peace a Chance" could be heard across the airwaves. In the six weeks after his death, more than two million copies of his records were sold in the UK alone, with "Imagine" passing the one-million mark.

Six months after the killing, George Harrison remembered John in "All of Those Years", paying his own poignant tribute to him in the lyrics: "But you point the way to the truth when you say/All you need is love".

Opposite bottom: It didn't take long for conspiracy theories to emerge about John's death, with suggestions that he had been the victim of a political assassination plot by US government agents; none of the claims have ever been substantiated.

JOHN LENNON TIMELINE: 1980-ONWARDS

1981

12 Jan US release of John's "Woman"/"Beautiful Boy (Darling Boy)" (16 Jan in the UK).

18 Jan Yoko responds to the messages of goodwill which she has received since John's death, by publishing a letter of gratitude in newspapers around the world.

18 Jan Radio 1 broadcasts the first of five programmes entitled *The Lennon Tapes*, airing the Andy Peebles interview of 6 December 1980.

20 Feb Yoko's only UK solo single, "Walking On Thin Ice" is released. She is interviewed on radio for the first time since John's death.

Mar An announcement is made that a forest is to be planted in Israel as a tribute to John.

Mar Paul publishes his tribute, which includes previously unseen photographs taken by his wife Linda.

13 Mar US release of "Watching The Wheels"/"Yes I'm Your Angel" (27 March in the UK).

29 Mar A memorial service for John is held in Liverpool.

11 May George releases a tribute single, "All Those Years Ago", featuring Paul and Ringo, in the US (15 May in the UK).

22 May Yoko makes her first official public appearance since John's death, accepting the Handel Medallion, New York's highest cultural accolade.

24 Aug John's murderer, Mark Chapman, is sentenced and jailed for a minimum term of twenty years, and a maximum of life imprisonment.

9 Oct Yoko proclaims this date, which would have been John's birthday, "International World Peace Day". A statue of John is unveiled in LA.

28 Oct *Lennon* the musical opens in Liverpool.

22 Dec Sotheby's hold the first major rock memorabilia auction in London, selling a small Lennon self-portrait for £8000.

1982

Jan The complete transcript of the extensive *Playboy* interview is published in book form.

24 Feb Yoko and Sean attend the Grammy Awards, collecting the best album award for *Double Fantasy.*

20 Apr An official ceremony is held in Central Park, New York, where Yoko announces the planning of a three-and-a-half acre site to be dedicated to John, named "Strawberry Fields".

1 Nov *The John Lennon Collection,* a compilation album, is released in the UK (8 Nov in the US).

13 Nov The first annual John Lennon Scholarship is awarded by George Martin on behalf of The Performing Rights Society.

15 Nov EMI release "Love" as a single.

1983

1 Sept The original hand-written lyrics for "Imagine" are sold at Sotheby's for £6500.

11 Sept The Peace Museum in Chicago exhibits a number of John's artefacts.

13 Oct John is posthumously awarded the Freedom of the City by Liverpool City Council.

5 Dec The LP *Heart Play – Unfinished Dialogue*, featuring John and Yoko's 1980 *Playboy* interview is released in the US (16 December in the UK).

1984

5 Jan US single release of "Nobody Told Me"/"O' Sanity" (9 Jan in the UK).

19 Jan US album release of John and Yoko's *Milk And Honey* (23 Jan in the UK).

13 Feb Pete Shotton publishes *John Lennon: In My Life*, an account of his friendship with John.

9 Mar UK single release of "Borrowed Time"/"Your Hands" (11 May in the US).

15 Mar US single release of "I'm Stepping Out"/"Sleepless Night" (15 Jul in the UK).

21 Mar Yoko officially opens the "Strawberry Fields" site in Central Park with Julian, Sean and mayor Ed Koch.

Apr An unauthorized double album, *Reflections And Poetry* is released in the UK. It contains part of the interview which John gave to RKO before his death. Yoko takes legal action and the album is withdrawn.

Jun Jon Weiner's *Come Together: John Lennon In His Time* is published. In it Weiner discusses Lennon's previously withheld FBI files.

5 Oct The single "Every Man Has A Woman Who Loves Him", backed by Sean Lennon singing "It's Alright", is released in the US (16 Nov in the UK).

1985

13 May John's uncle Charles unveils a new British Rail engine named "John Lennon", for the London to Liverpool route.

9 Oct Yoko and Sean open a garden on the "Strawberry Fields" site, Central Park, New York.

2 Nov The stage play *Lennon* opens in London.

18 Nov "Jealous Guy" is issued by EMI as a single.

6 Dec A collection of John's hand-written letters and lyrics go on display in the manuscripts room of the British Museum, on loan from Beatles' biographer, Hunter Davies.

1986

24 Jan US release of LP *John Lennon: Live In New York City* (24 Feb UK).

21 Mar Yoko appears at Wembley Conference Centre, London, as part of her "Star Peace Tour".

6 Oct A book of John's previously unreleased writings and drawings are published, entitled *Skywriting By Word Of Mouth*.

27 Oct US release of LP *Menlove Avenue*, containing previously unreleased recordings by John (3 Nov in the UK).

8 Dec Czech police disperse hundreds of fans gathered for a public memorial service to John in Prague.

1987

4 Apr The first John Lennon New Age Award is awarded to promoter Bill Graham at the New York Music Awards. It is presented by Yoko.

24 Apr A ballet based upon the album *John Lennon / The Plastic Ono Band*, entitled *The Dream Is Over* opens in London.

1988

20 Jan The Beatles are added to the Rock and Roll Hall of Fame at an award ceremony held at the Waldorf Astoria in New York. George, Ringo, Yoko, Julian and Sean attend.

11 Jul UK-only release of *The Last Word*, consisting of part of the interview with John at RKO.

19 Sept The preview of *Imagine*, a new Lennon art exhibition, is attended by Yoko at London's Business Design Centre.

30 Sept Yoko unveils John's star on the Hollywood Walk of Fame, outside the Capitol Records building.

4 Oct US release of CD/LP *Imagine: John Lennon* (10 Oct in the UK).

28 Oct The documentary film *Imagine: John Lennon* opens in London. Three years were spent making the film which was authorized by Yoko, and as such, the producers had been granted unlimited access to the Lennon Estate's collection of footage, much of which had previously been unseen by the public.

1989

Jul *The Murder Of John Lennon* is published by Fenton Bresler, a British journalist and barrister, in which he claims CIA involvement in John's assassination.

Sept Bag One Gallery is opened by Yoko Ono in New York, selling expensive "official" Lennon merchandise.

1990

25 Mar The Amsterdam Hilton re-opens room 209 on the 21st anniversary of John and Yoko's "bed-in" there. The room is given the title, "The John and Yoko Honeymoon Suite".

1 Oct A CD boxed set of John's songs from 1969–1980 is released by EMI as *Lennon*.

9 Oct The 50th anniversary of John's birth is marked by a ceremony at the New York United Nations Building, featuring a short speech by Yoko, a recording of John talking about peace, and the playing of *Imagine*. The event is broadcast live, world-wide.

7 Dec The 10th anniversary of John's death, and the 50th anniversary of his birth, are honoured in Liverpool by the lord mayor unveiling the first official plaque for John in his hometown.

14 Dec UK release of *Testimony*, a longer version of the RKO interview.

1991

Jan With impending military action by the UN against Iraq, "Give Peace A Chance" is recorded by Yoko and Sean with Lenny Kravitz. The single is released in the UK on the 28th, but is met by a BBC ban.

20 Feb A Lifetime Achievement Award granted posthumously to John, is collected by Yoko at the 33rd Grammy Awards ceremony.

12 Jul The FBI is instructed by a US court to release sixty-nine documents concerning John Lennon, which it had previously withheld on the grounds of "national interest".

6 Dec John's Aunt Mimi dies aged eighty-eight at the Dorset home bought for her by John in 1965.

1992

15 Jul A new Lennon musical opens in Liverpool, also titled *Imagine*.

Oct The play *Looking Through A Glass Onion – John Lennon In Words And Music*, runs in London for just a few days.

5 Oct *The John Lennon Video Collection* is released by a subsidiary of EMI.

1993

17 Apr Yoko holds an exhibition in LA which includes a replica, in bronze, of the broken spectacles that John was wearing when he was killed.

1994

Jan John is posthumously entered into The Rock and Roll Hall of Fame in New York as a solo artist by Paul McCartney. During a press conference with Paul and Sean, Yoko gives Paul a copy of the unfinished song "Free as a Bird", with the intention that it may be completed by the remaining Beatles, to be included in *The Beatles' Anthology*, Apple's new CD and television project.

30 Nov A double Beatles CD, *Live At The BBC* is released by EMI. Six million copies are sold within six months.

1995

Feb "Real Love", a second unfinished Lennon composition, is completed by Paul, George and Ringo.

19 Nov *The Beatles Anthology* is shown on US television and includes the new "Beatles" track "Free as a Bird".

21 Nov Release of *The Beatles Anthology 1*, the first in a series of three double albums of unreleased out-takes and mixes.

4 Dec "Free as a Bird" is released as a single, reaching No. 2 in the UK charts.

1996

4 Mar "Real Love" is released as a single.

18 Mar *The Beatles Anthology 2* is released.

28 Oct *The Beatles Anthology 3* is released.

1997

20 Jun Yoko collects a posthumous award for John in London, recognizing his outstanding contribution to British music.

25 Sept Eighty pages from the FBI's Lennon files are released as The American Civil Liberties Union, representing author Jon Weiner, win their case. Weiner is later to publish his findings in his book, *Gimme Some Truth: The John Lennon FBI files*.

27 Oct Release of CD/LP *Lennon Legend: The Very Best Of John Lennon* (23 Feb 1998 in the US).

1998

2 Nov UK release of the four-CD set *The John Lennon Anthology*, containing over 100 previously unreleased tracks (3 Nov in the US).

1 Dec Yoko briefly revives the campaign she and John began in 1969, unveiling a "War Is Over" poster in Times Square, New York.

1999

Apr John Lennon is voted "the greatest rock singer of all time" in a *Mojo* magazine readers' poll.

1 Aug John Lennon is ranked at number one in a *Q Magazine* readers' poll of the top 100 Greatest Stars of The 20th Century.

2002

A 100 Greatest Britons BBC poll votes Lennon into eighth place.

2004

Acoustic, a compilation album of John Lennon demos, studio and live performances that feature his acoustic guitar work, is released.

Rolling Stone magazine ranks John Lennon No. 38 on its list of The Immortals: The Fifty Greatest Artists of All Time.

2006

Sept *The US Versus John Lennon*, a documentary dealing with John Lennon's transformation from a member of The Beatles to an anti-war activist is released. The film also details the attempts by the United States government to silence him.

2006

Dec The final ten documents in Lennon's FBI file reporting on his ties with London anti-war activists in 1971 are released.

2008

Rolling Stone magazine ranks Lennon No. 5 on its list of 100 Greatest Singers of All Time.

Nov In a newspaper article, the *Vatican* forgives John for his "more popular than Jesus" remarks made in 1966.

2009

July Lennon's 1958 Hofner Senator guitar sells for £205,250 at auction.

Dec *Nowhere Boy*, the biopic of John's adolescence, is released. Directed by Sam Taylor-Wood, it had received its world premiere two months earlier at the closing night of the London Film Festival.

2010

June Lennon's handwritten lyrics for "A Day In The Life" sell at auction for $1.2 million.

Oct The John Lennon Peace Monument is unveiled at a ceremony in Liverpool by Julian and Cynthia Lennon to celebrate what would have been John's 70th birthday.

Oct Yoko Ono unveils an English Heritage blue plaque at 34 Montagu Square, the first home she and John shared in London.

Oct Google releases an animated tribute to John on the eve of the 30th anniversary of his death.

2011

June A copy of *Double Fantasy*, signed by Lennon hours before he was shot, sells at auction in London for £23,750.

2012

June The Beatles are named as the biggest-selling singles act since Queen Elizabeth II acceded to the throne.

2013

Sept Five Beatles' albums *Help!*, *Rubber Soul*, *Revolver*, *The Beatles (White Album)* and *Abbey Road* – are granted platinum status in the UK, having sold more than 300,000 copies. *Sgt Pepper's Lonely Hearts Club Band* is granted triple platinum status; it had sold over 900,000 copies since 1994 and an estimated 5.1 million copies since its release in 1967.

2015

April Cynthia Lennon dies.

Nov Lennon's Gibson J-160E guitar (played by him on "Love Me Do") is sold at auction for $2.4million.

2016

March George Martin dies.

Sept The premiere of *The Beatles: Eight Days A Week – The Touring Years* is shown at London's Leicester Square Odeon.

2017

June Yoko Ono receives a song-writing credit on "Imagine".

2019

Sept The 50th anniversary reissue of *Abbey Road* is released. Giles Martin – son of George Martin – produced the album.

2020

9 Oct The 80th anniversary of John's birth.

8 Dec The 40th anniversary of John's death.

Yoko and Sean in 1984 outside Strawberry Field in Liverpool, where she announced she had made a donation of $90,000 to the Salvation Army children's home. The orphanage, the inspiration for "Strawberry Fields Forever", closed in 2005, reopening as a prayer centre shortly afterwards.

Credits

The pictures in this book are from the archives of Associated Newspapers. Additional photographs to complement this celebration of the life of John Lennon have been provided by Getty Images. Particular thanks to Steve Torrington, Dave Shepherd, Brian Jackson, Alan Pinnock, Paul Rossiter, Richard Jones and all the staff at Associated Newspapers without whose help this book would not have been possible.

All images © Associated Newspapers except for the following, which are © Getty Images.

(T = Top; B = Bottom; L = Left; R = Right):

1, 3, 4, 10, 11, 12, 13, 15, 17, 19, 22, 74, 96, 103, 104, 106b, 107, 109t, 116, 122, 129, 130, 153, 158, 162, 168, 173tr, 196t, 198, 209, 210, 211b, 212, 213t&b, 214, 215t,&b, 216 inset, 217

P. 50. (Fred Lennon): http://proxy.handle.net/10648/aae0e0fe-d0b4-102d-bcf8-003048976d84

p. 223 B. Farrel from Daily Mail Archive

P. 170t: Joost Evers

© Robert Whitaker: Front Cover and page 95

Bibliography

The Beatles, H. Davies (Arrow, London, 1992)

The John Lennon Encyclopedia, B. Harry (Virgin, London, 2000)

We All Shine On, P. Du Noyer (Carlton Books, London, 1997)

The Complete Beatles Chronicle, M. Lewisohn (Hamlyn, London, 2000)

Icons of Rock: John Lennon   A story in Photographs, T. Burrows (Bookmart, London, 2000)

Lennon, The Definitive Biography, R. Coleman (Pan, London, 2000)

Let Me Take You Down, J. Jones, (Virgin, London, 1993)

Last Interview, All We are Saying, D. Sheff, (Pan, London, 2001)